# DERBY GIRL

# DERBY GIRL
## A MEMOIR

by Sammi Jones

 **NDSU** NORTH DAKOTA STATE
UNIVERSITY PRESS

Dept. 2360, P.O. Box 6050, Fargo, ND 58108-6050
www.ndsu.edu/ahss/ndirs

# Derby Girl: A Memoir

© 2017 by North Dakota State University Press
First Edition

ISBN: 978-0-911042-97-9
Library of Congress Control Number: 2017930228

Cover design by Jamie Hohnadel Trosen
Interior design by Deb Tanner
Author photo by Jen Krook
Derby 101 images by Cruel of Thirds and Shayli Johnson

The publication of *Derby Girl: A Memoir* is made possible by the generous support of donors to the NDSU Press Fund and the NDSU Press Endowment Fund.

For copyright permission, please contact Suzzanne Kelley at 701-231-6848 or suzzanne.kelley@ndsu.edu.

Kent Sandstrom, Director
Suzzanne Kelley, Editor in Chief
Editorial Intern, Angela Beaton

Publishing Interns for *Derby Girl: A Memoir*
Constance Bina-Economos, Samuel Caspers, Ashley Hegeholz, Sydney Olstad

Printed in Canada

A catalog record for this book is available from Quality Books, Inc.
http://www.quality-books.com/

∞ This paper meets the requirements of ANSI/NISO Z39.48-1992 (Permanence of Paper).

 **NDSU** NORTH DAKOTA STATE UNIVERSITY PRESS

Dept. 2360, P.O. Box 6050, Fargo, ND 58108-6050
www.ndsu.edu/ahss/ndirs

*for my biological family and my derby family*

# TIMEOUT: DERBY 101
# TURN THREE: MAJORS

# TURN FOUR: CALLING OFF THE JAM

# GLOSSARY OF DERBY-NESS

Acknowledgements

About the Author

About the Press

## Author's Note

This is a work of creative nonfiction. The events are portrayed to the best of my memory. While all stories in this book are true, some names and identifying details have been changed to protect the privacy of the people involved.

# Prologue

Nobody wakes up one morning and says, *Gee, I think I'll move to Fargo*. Out of all the people I know in the Fargo-Moorhead area, 99 percent of them reside there because they were bribed into moving there.

While finishing the super-senior year of my undergraduate studies in tropical St. Cloud, Minnesota, I had no idea what I wanted to do with my life. Who does when they're twenty-three? And what does one do with a degree in Creative Writing and a minor in Communication Studies? I had no desire to get out into the real world because that meant I'd have to work (sigh) AND pay back my student loans (extra sigh).

So I decided to cast a line into the Master of Fine Arts in Creative Writing whirlpool to see if I got any nibbles. I sent my applications and writing samples to a few MFA programs around the Midwest and even Colorado. Rejection letters flooded my email inbox and my parents' real mailbox at my home address. Throughout the early spring months of 2008, I moped around Saint Cloud State University's campus and the local downtown pubs like a pitiful Dostoyevsky character in need of clean clothes and a pat on the back. Then, out of the blue, the sweet baby Jesus put the kibosh on my pity-party by making the professors at Minnesota State University Moorhead send me an acceptance email into the MFA program. The day I opened my inbox a heavenly choir of angels sang out, and before I could say *uff-dah* I was on my way to Fargo.

During my first two years in the program I was immersed in creative writing workshops, British literature classes, my graduate assistant job, and bottomless pitchers of beer. My fellow grad buddies and I discussed everyone from Whitman to the Brontë sisters to Faulkner. We frequented local bars, our favorite being the Knights of Columbus, where the beer was lukewarm and the popcorn tasted like Styrofoam. We stayed out all night because the following day's workshop wasn't until 6 p.m. We wrote, we discussed, we drank, and then we drank some more.

The Fargo-Moorhead area wasn't half-bad. Sure there were the occasional thirty-below January nights, wicked blizzards that led to city-wide shut downs, and forty-foot-deep flood waters that led apartments to boast of ocean-side views. But minus those matters, life was okay, even tolerable. But something was missing. I couldn't put my thumb on it. And then I found it. Or it found me.

# TURN ONE: THE FIRST TEN THOUSAND LAPS

# Fargo Has Derby?

It started with a newspaper ad. "Fargo has roller derby?" I say to no one in particular at the bar on a frigid February night in 2010. I fold the *High Plains Reader* and stare at the ad depicting a cartoonish bad-ass girl on skates. My jaw is halfway submerged in my lukewarm Miller Lite while I repeat, "Fargo has roller derby?"

A few people I'm out with say that they've seen ads before but have never actually been downtown to watch it. Someone else chimes in saying she's heard it's difficult to get tickets because the games always sell out.

"Well jeeze, how come I didn't know about this? I wanna play roller derby."

A few of my friends roll their eyes while others practically spit their drinks across the table.

"What?" I ask, looking around.

My friend takes a sip of his beer, sets it down, leans over to me and says, "Those girls are huge . . . you'd TOTALLY get KILLED!"

That summer I decide to play softball for a local bar in Fargo, and to my great surprise our pitcher turns out to be (gasp) a Fargo-Moorhead Derby Girl. Though she towers over my five-feet-four-inch stature by a good six inches and could easily pulverize my one-hundred-fifteen-pound body into a two-by-three-foot slab of road kill, such trivial matters don't stop my hounding her with roller derby questions. *What is roller derby? How are the games played? They're not called "games"; they're called "bouts"? How many girls are on the team? Oh, there are different teams within the league? Are the skaters all as big as you? How do you hit? You can't use elbows? What kind of gear do you need? Can you play without insurance? Do you think I could play derby? Tryouts are in July at Skateland?*

"Wait a minute, you're doing what?" Lonny Blossoms sets his cold glass of beer on the table.

"I'm trying out for roller derby tonight," I say through a half-crooked smile.

He continues to look at me with his notorious thinking face — one I've witnessed a lot over the past two years. Tall, broad-shouldered and burly, his appearance is a cross between a linebacker, a secret service agent, and a boxer. His head is bald and when he opens his mouth a thick Northeastern accent rolls off his tongue. Besides his name, nothing about Lonny Blossoms screams poet.

"I didn't think you were actually serious about trying out for roller derby," Lonny says, looking me in the eye.

"Of course I was serious. I need something else to do and I miss being part of a team. I loved being on the golf team during my undergrad, and I've always been in sports. I need to try something new for a bit."

"All right, all right," Lonny holds up his hands, "I know you're gonna do what you're gonna do. Just don't get killed."

"Seriously, you're like the billionth person who's said that to me today."

"Well you do have a pretty little face there, Sammi Jones," he laughs in his high-pitched chuckle and downs his last sip of beer.

I grin. "You're a real smart ass."

"You gonna have another beer?" he sets his empty glass on the table.

"Nope, I don't want to be all schnockered up before tryouts tonight."

# The First Lap

I arrive at Skateland forty-five minutes before tryouts are scheduled to begin. Walking into the building I'm greeted by a cool, air-conditioned atmosphere that smells like Big Red cinnamon gum. I approach a booth where two girls wearing derby t-shirts sit organizing papers. Because I've seen their photos on the FMDG's website (a site I've been stalking for the last month) I recognize one as Jinja Turtle and the other as Charred Coating.

"Are you here for tryouts?" Charred Coating's pen hovers over a sheet of paper. She looks at me with a partial grin, as if hiding something besides the rest of her marvelously straight white teeth.

I nod my head in agreement and say my name.

"Oh, you're the Sammi who sent me the email asking for tryout information."

I smile, nod again, and recollect that in her email reply the word *helmet* had been spelled *helmut*, which had caused me to wonder if too many derby hits eventually led to a complete disregard for Microsoft Spell Check.

I rent a pair of tired looking tan skates equipped with bright orange wheels that don't feel or look much different from painted rocks. While I haven't been on roller skates for God knows how long, I *had* earlier that day rummaged through my Christmas decorations, golf accessories, and long forgotten winter sweaters to find at the bottom of the heap my trusty purple roller blades from junior high. And while the blades had felt a bit tighter than I remembered, I was able to complete a short spin around my south Fargo neighborhood with zero wipeouts — a sure sign I was ready to play roller derby.

"Oh shit," I mutter as I finally stand in the laced-up rentals. Unsure whether it's easier to walk or skate across the carpeted area, I grab a metal railing to pull myself toward the rink and down onto the hardwood floor. There are already a handful of derby girls out on the track skating in a counterclockwise circle. Decked out in helmets, knee pads, elbow pads, and wrist guards, they appear to be as cool with skating as Rod Blagojevich is with selling Obama's senate seat. An overwhelming desire to be like them kicks into gear and, trying to gain control of my shaky legs, I release my death grip on the railing and coast onto the track.

A derby girl skates up to me and offers a friendly hello. I try to look up to return the greeting but swiveling my head disrupts my concentration and nearly lands me on my ass.

"How do you skate so fast?" I ask the derby girl, my eyes glued to the floor while trying to find a fluid skating motion.

"I've practiced for a while," she replies as we merge toward the center of the track. "Trust me, it just takes time."

Our leader for the evening introduces herself as Lieutenant Lutefist or Lutefist for short. She welcomes us new girls with genuine warmth and gratitude so I figure she's sweet and harmless — especially because she sports a large and colorful ice cream sundae tattoo on her arm. However, within seconds of beginning the first drill, somebody flips the crazy switch on Lutefist and she begins screaming, "SKATE FASTER DAMMIT!" All of us new girls exchange nervous glances with one another and express a common "oh my GOD!" with our eyes.

As tryouts progress I'm mesmerized by some of the new girls who have complete control over their skates. They seem to possess mad Nancy Kerrigan skills — whirling and twirling around the rink like they're floating on some fluffy angelic cloud — while all I seem to possess is a pair of demonic skates that enjoy driving me into either the Pollockesque carpeted wall at the far end of the rink or the steel blue railing at the near.

Three-quarters of the way through tryouts I get cocky during a drill the derby girls call the 25 in 5* and think *ooh yeah, I've made ten laps around the track . . . I've TOTALLY got the hang of this skating business.* Just as I lift my head up to look at nobody in particular, my right foot quivers and veers north toward Winnipeg, my left foot takes a southwest route toward Tucson, and I topple forward in what must look like a slow-motioned Hollywood "I've-been-shot!" stupor. A harmonic "OOOhhh!" crescendos from the chorus of seasoned players as I squeal to a bare-kneed halt on the polished wood floor.

At the end of the grueling three-hour LONG tryout session, I'm left with achy wrists, bruises in places I didn't know could bruise, a bad case of tinnitus from Lieutenant Lutefist's screaming, and a burning hatred for the rental skates that have undoubtedly caused irreversible nerve damage to my feet and my ego.

Outside of Skateland a nervous energy hangs in the mid-July evening air. I smile when I meet the eyes of a fellow competitor but shy away from engaging in any light chatter. I'm certain I haven't made the team since three-quarters of the girls trying out actually knew how to skate *and* stop — a winning combination in my eyes.

After what seems like an eternity, Lutefist and the other FMDG skaters who helped to evaluate tryouts exit Skateland and join us in the parking lot to announce the results. In a half-grimaced state of anticipation, I wait for Lutefist's "SKATE-FASTER-DAMMIT!" voice to crack the air, but to mine and

* An asterisk indicates a term you might want to look up in the Glossary of Derbyness, located at the back of this book.

everyone else's surprise she addresses us using an inside voice — even though we're all outside — and we now find ourselves inching closer to her cautiously, the way one would approach a firecracker that didn't go off.

"Well, as you're all aware, there are thirteen spots available to fill in the league and twenty of you tried out. Naturally, seven of you should be sent home. However, after looking over everybody's charts and taking into consideration that 40 percent of you probably won't survive past two weeks of practice, we've decided to take all of you."

Cheers and laughter rocket skyward, but I'm unable to participate in the excitement because my jaw is nearly resting on the pavement in a you've-got-to-be-kidding-me state of awe and bewilderment.

"Congratulations!" Lutefist yells in her familiar loud voice. "You're now derby girls! Welcome to FMDG!"

# Butch Lesbians

The first thing my sister says to me over the phone when I tell her I made the Fargo-Moorhead derby team is, "What!? They're all a bunch of butch lesbians!" I'm not quite sure how to reply to the statement. I expected my sister, Jen, to be a little less direct since she was the most open-minded person in my family. There was no, "Whoa, congrats Sam, that's awesome!" or, "Sweet, way to try something new, sista!"

I decide my best reply is an "Ugh, whatever," because I'm sitting in my steamy car (the air conditioner is broken) outside my ghetto apartment (the cell phone reception in my basement efficiency is terrible), uncomfortable in my sweat-drenched clothes, and now irritated by Jen's response. I didn't actually know any of the skaters — newbies or seasoned players — but they didn't *all* look like a bunch of butch lesbians. But then again, what does a butch lesbian look like? And who's to say one person's butch is the other's butch? And what exactly is *wrong* with a bunch of butch lesbians? My sister was making derby sound like some sort of taboo club only Jerry Springer would be willing to investigate.

I hear a faraway, "Oh NOW what'd she do?" on the other end of the phone and, until now, I'd forgotten Mom was at my sister and brother-in-law's house for a few days every week during the summer to watch the kids. Mom gets on the phone and asks, "What?" a dozen times. It's not her way of saying "I can't hear you"; it's her way of saying "I don't agree with what you've done." She reminds me that I don't have health insurance, and finishes with, "How are you planning to pay for this *new idea*?"

And to top off the conversation, when my sister gets back on the phone she tells me John (her husband) has just described roller derby to my eleven- and eight-year-old niece and nephew and they've both agreed "Sam's gonna get killed."

# Interjections

When talking with Mom, any time I begin a conversation with a long drawn out, "So . . ." my voice is immediately run over, flattened out, then backed over again by Mom's dump-truck-esque interjection of, "Oh now what'd you do!?" Somehow, the way she says it, her interjection never really sounds like a question, nor does it sound like a statement. Rather, it's more of a mix between a threat and a demand — basically her way of coming to terms with the fact that, once again, I screwed something up. Examples:

> Me: "So . . ."
> Mom: "Oh now what'd you do?"
> Me: "The state patrol gave me a ticket for going
> ninety in a seventy zone! Isn't THAT ridiculous?"

>> Or

> Me: "So . . ."
> Mom: "Oh now what'd you do?"
> Me: "I dropped my cell phone in the toilet!" (Mom
> still thinks The Great Dunk was an evil scheme I
> carried out so I could get a new phone.)

>> Or

> Me: "So . . ."
> Mom: "Oh now what'd you do?"
> Me: "I'm transferring colleges. I started taking anti-

depressants. I got another traffic ticket for suppos-
edly running a stop sign. I overdrew my checking
account. I'm transferring back to my first college. I
quit the golf team. I got too many parking tickets
on campus and now they won't let me register for
classes until I pay the bill. I crashed the car. I got
arrested. I joined ROLLER DERBY! I hurt my ankle
at derby practice. I banged up the new car. I got a
dog. My unpaid medical bills got sent to collections.
I overdrew my checking account . . . again."

# Three Reasons Why I Should Play Roller Derby

**#1: I can do anything on wheels.**

In the nineties, rollerblading was in (and roller skating was out). Around third grade my first pair of blades arrived via the Easter Bunny. They were black with green laces and had one adjustable clicky strap near the top of the boot. That summer I tested their versatility and discovered that all of the most important things in life could still be done while wearing rollerblades. I could play driveway hockey, tennis, basketball, soccer, Frisbee, catch, tag, and (one of my personal favorite games) chase-the-little-multi-colored-bouncy-ball-down-the-street. I could climb and do flips off the monkey bars, run through the sprinkler, climb up the rope attached to the tree, take shortcuts through neighbors' backyards, take the dog out, race remote control cars, build Lego towers, and flood the sandbox—all while wearing rollerblades.

When first getting used to my blades, I remember that having to come inside to use the bathroom posed a huge problem. Mom hated me clunking down the stairs in my blades — "Samantha Marie you sound like a herd of elephants!"— and leaving wheel tracks on the carpet. Personally, I hated having to sit down, unclick, untie, and pull off my blades, run downstairs to use the bathroom, then run back upstairs, pull on my blades, tie, click, and get back outside. So I decided to meet Mom in the middle. Okay, not really in the middle, more toward my side. I would sneak into the porch, dust off my wheels, then tiptoe inside down the stairs and into the bathroom, do my thing, then tiptoe back up the stairs, out the door (without letting it slam) and be on my merry way. From there on out I realized it was even possible to be a secret undercover agent while still wearing rollerblades.

#### #2: No fear of falling.

I don't ever remember being afraid to fall, probably because I'd never, and still have never, broken a bone. According to Mom, the doctor always said I had abnormally loose joints, which equaled more bend and less snap. I don't ever remember wearing any sort of protective gear — no helmet, knee pads, or wrist guards. Sure, I had my fair share of scraped-up knees and elbows from trying to master some stupid trick like, *Will the release of the plastic grocery bag parachute be able to stop the pretzel bent skater weaving down the hill?* or, *Is it possible to hit the GI Joe figure with a Nerf gun bullet from a midair position after liftoff from a homemade ramp?* In the end, the scrapes and bruises never really bothered me.

#### #3: I'm damn stubborn.

I had some wicked good ideas that led to some wicked good bruises and bleeding wounds. But, reflecting over this now, it's strange that I don't ever remember Mom being mad or reprimanding me whenever I'd come home looking for a Band-Aid. Mom had always been overprotective of her children — to the point that it's the eighth wonder of the world why the Jones kids didn't smother to death from extreme overprotection. When Mom and Dad purchased their first microwave, Mom read the manual cover to cover and wouldn't let my brother or sister into the kitchen while it was running because, "You don't know what sort of radiation it gives off." Even in the nineties, whenever I'd glance into the microwave to check the status of a cheese sandwich, Mom would holler, "Don't look in there, it's bad for your eyes!"

So why didn't Mom get mad at me for coming home bruised, battered, and bleeding after each rollerblading disaster? Why didn't she sternly ask, "Samantha Marie, what in the world have you been doing?" And why did she let me leave the house without wearing even so much as a helmet? Many MANY moons later, while on the phone with Mom, I ask her these questions, and she responds, "Well, we had the knee pads and everything for you in the front closet, but you refused to wear them . . . [sigh]. . . even *then*, you were just like your father — so damn stubborn. I got tired of arguing with you and figured oh, what the hell; they were your knees anyway."

# A Pricey Intuition

While shopping for derby gear, I can practically hear a little version of Mom sitting on my shoulder spitting into my ear, "How are you gonna pay for all this!?" As I wander around the derby gear section at Tubs of Fun (a pool/hot-tub/billiards-we-sell-EVERYTHING-sort-of-store owned by a Merby* skater, I can't help but recall the weird feeling I'd experienced during tryouts. At some point during the evening — somewhere between crashing into the carpeted wall at the end of the track and face-planting onto the floor — a spark I'd long figured had deserted me abruptly sputtered and fizzled to life. It's difficult to describe this spark because it's not something tangible to watch flicker, play around with, or examine under a microscope. It's a feeling that tingles throughout your body and makes the hairs on the back of your neck stand up. It's the sensation of butterflies while opening a Christmas gift from Santa. It's the realization that a tree dormant and blanketed by an apocalyptic amount of snow will eventually come back to life in the spring. It's the sheer ecstasy of finding just one more can of Mountain Dew in the back of the refrigerator. It's an intuition, a gut-deep feeling that whispers to you, "This is it, this is right, you're on to something."

It was the same feeling I had experienced in seventh grade while trying to hit a golf ball for the first time. The same feeling I'd experienced during my first creative writing class senior year of my undergrad. Though I'd only felt this spark a few times, it had led to positive life-altering events. It was enough to grab my attention at Skateland and, at this moment, enough to make me drop $300 on brand new derby gear.

I sit in my apartment that night noting the differences between my new Riedell R3 quad skates and my beat up rollerblades. One major difference is the boot itself. As opposed to bulky roller-blade boots that extend halfway up the shin, quad boots cut off around the ankle. *A more flexible ankle will be a good thing, right?*

Next, because they have two wheels on the outside of the boot and two on the inside, quad skates look more sturdy and stable. When left unattended blades topple over, but quad skates remain upright on their own. *So they should be easier to balance in, right?*

The last big difference I notice between quad skates and blades is the location of the brakes. Instead of hanging off the heel (as on blades) the brakes on quads hang off the toe area. The toe stops themselves are dainty compared to the stoppers on the back of my blades, but, thinking about it, when moving forward it should be easier to slow down by dragging your toe rather than your heel. The toe drag seemed to work well in football when a receiver needed to slow down to catch a ball in bounds. *Derby was practically football on wheels, right?*

How much different could these quad skates be from my roll-erblades? The skates I'd rented during tryouts had been difficult to get the hang of, but that was because they had been ancient, a product from a different millennium — a good idea but not fully thought out and primed before retail, like lawn darts. I bet all of the wobbling and falling and crashing into walls during tryouts was because of those Skateland skates. It hadn't been that *I* didn't know how to skate, it had been that *those skates* didn't know how to skate.

# Drift Prairie Cleaners

With school being done for the summer, my graduate assistant job is nonexistent. In order to scrape by along the usual sandy bottom of my existence, I manage to snag a job cleaning houses. The business — Drift Prairie Cleaners — boasts of eco-friendly cleaning products that vow to keep your home living environment free of nasty foreign chemicals. Diane, the owner, is a fifty-something recently divorced woman who drives a pontoon-size maroon Lincoln with peeling paint and a Drift Prairie Cleaners logo slapped on the back window. She has a knack for cleaning and an overabundance of spray bottles full of toilet cleaner, vinegar, "special" cleaner — which seems to be a mix of water and vinegar — and air freshener that smells like orange Tic Tacs.

The cleaning crew consists of Diane, a woman named Marla, myself, and two other girls also in their twenties. While cleaning toilets and scrubbing leftover spaghetti sauce off kitchen countertops aren't my areas of expertise, there are a few nice perks to the job.

1. I can get away with wearing my ultimate favorite attire — grungy pit-stained t-shirts, running shorts, and running shoes. It takes me all of ten minutes to get ready for work in the morning.
2. On days when my "happy pills" aren't working, it's okay for me to crank up my iPod and drift away into a con-

glomeration of daydreams while mindlessly scrubbing a kitchen floor.

3. I can get my animal fix by befriending clients' dogs, cats, guinea pigs, rabbits, and even an un-hatched chicken in an incubator. Usually, when I'm in need of some animal time I announce to my co-workers that I'm taking out the garbage, which is actually code for "I'm going out to the garage to pet the dog."

# Coach Mahony

He is a mystical Canadian god who, when spoken of by skaters, is praised so highly that one would venture to guess he possesses a holy slab of stone etched with secrets to the derby world. "Oh, did you hear Coach *Mahony* is going to be in town?" "Oh, that Coach *Mahony*, he's a legend in the derby world." "*Coach Mahony . . . Mahony . . . MAAA-HO-NNYYY!*" With all the Mahony commotion, I can't help but picture a beefy Greek guy sporting a toga and an olive branch wrapped around his head.

Somehow FMDG is able to lure Coach Mahony across borders and down into Fargo for a derby boot camp weekend. As new girls, we're invited to attend both eight-hour camps Saturday and Sunday and told it will be a great learning environment. What we're not told is that it'll be a great learning environment only if we've already mastered the Blades2Quads* transition, understand the rules of roller derby, and have been skating in bouts for at least a year.

On Saturday I arrive at the large Urban Plains Center arena around noon — just in time for the second four-hour session. A sitting crowd of skaters is formed in the middle of the arena floor listening to the famous Coach Mahony preach something about hip checks. Mahony is somewhat like I had imagined — short and beefy — but wearing shorts and a t-shirt instead of a toga and an olive branch. I take a seat on a hockey bench near one of the seasoned skaters who sits in a wheelchair with her broken leg propped up. I dig through my giant bag of gear packed with brand-spankin'-new hundred-dollar R3 quad skates and a buffet of new protective gear: wrist guards, elbow pads, knee pads, a helmet, and a mouth guard.

It takes me a while to figure out how to put on all my gear laces, snaps, wraps, and Velcros, yet when I finish Coach Mahony is STILL talking. I sit on the bench and debate whether or not I should attempt to skate out onto the middle of the track and join up with the attentively listening group of skaters. I lean over to the skater in the wheelchair and ask, in a whisper, what I should do next.

"Go out and skate around to get warmed up," she says with a smile.

"Right now?" I whisper back, "In the middle of the talking?"

"Yes, yes, it's okay, just go out and skate around," she nods.

I'm not sure this is a good idea. Aside from the incessant baritone mumbling of Coach Mahony, the arena's atmosphere is that of a library. With skates on my feet my movement is as unpredictable as the Dow Jones Industrial Average, and any wrong shift in weight would for sure result in a loud and embarrassing Fourth of July sounding bang. I bite down on my mouth guard, try to let go of my ego, and delicately step onto the polished cement surface. I let out a little gasp because of how smooth the R3s feel compared to Skateland's rentals. *See Sam*, I think to myself, *the rentals were the reason you couldn't skate.*

Just as I make my second loop around the track, Coach Mahony decides he's done talking and that it's time for drills. The skaters stand up off the floor and I maneuver my way toward the group. Forgetting that I don't know how to stop, I bump into one person, another, and another while lisping through my mouth guard, "Thharrry, I don't know how to thtop yet!" before finally crashing into the arena's hockey boards. (Note to self: *it wasn't the rentals.*)

Later that afternoon, while falling in all directions compatible with a compass, I'm happy to notice that I'm not the only new girl at boot camp who is struggling to figure out the basics of roller derby. A few other skaters I had seen during tryouts were also here trying to figure out the whole ordeal. By observing the seasoned skaters the basics of roller derby appear to be:

1.   Skating fast
2.   Hitting while skating fast
3.   Hitting while being hit while skating fast
4.   Staying upright while hitting while being hit while skating fast

However, to us new girls — referred to as Fresh Meat*— our basics of roller derby appear to be:

1.   Falling
2.   Getting hit and falling
3.   Trying to hit and falling
4.   Not getting hit and falling
5.   Falling in the midst of a falling fall

Sunday night after Coach Mahony's boot camp I'm sore, frustrated, and a mixture of cranky and excited. Though I had just spent 99 percent of my weekend lying face down on a concrete floor, had a pulsating bruise the size of a bowling ball on my thigh, and didn't have enough ice packs or prescription meds to numb my aches and pains, I still felt a twinge of excitement while thinking about roller derby.

Over the weekend it was as if I'd been whisked away to another planet entirely, one where people skated at lightning fast speeds, hit the shit out of each other, pummeled to the ground, got up like nothing happened, and did it all over again. It seemed like the seasoned derby skaters had it all — stamina, guts, athleticism, and confidence. I was envious.

What grabbed my attention the most during Coach Mahony's boot camp was when he gathered all the skaters around for a session he liked to call: "You Suck." After watching us for the past two days he had made mental notes of each individual skater, assessing her strengths and weaknesses. "You Suck" was his way of getting across to each skater what she needed to work on. Instead of pulling each of us aside to talk privately (the polite way to tell someone they suck), Mahony said his two cents to each individual in front of the entire group. He didn't hold back and was blunt and direct toward every skater, some of whom looked rather startled and taken aback by his comments toward them. His criticisms were all over the board ranging from, "You need to get rid of your bad attitude" to "You need to get your ass to the gym." When Coach Mahony had finally gotten to me, he'd looked me in the eye and said in a simple matter-of-fact tone, "You need to learn how to skate. After that you'll be just fine."

# A Burning Desire

"I just don't understand why you want to play *roller derby*," Mom sighs over the phone, "Why in the world would you want to hit anybody?"

It's evening and I'm lying in bed with one ice pack wrapped around my knee and another resting on my massive thigh bruise.

"Ahh," I pause, "Because it's fun. I always told you I wanted to play hockey when I was little, but you never let me," I groan, trying to find a comfortable position.

"Because it was dangerous and it wasn't something I wanted you doing," Mom firmly states.

"Which is probably why I have this burning desire to play roller derby now . . . because you never let me get it out of my system when I was little."

After a brief silence Mom continues, "Well, I just don't understand why everything is always my fault. You kids all played sports growing up. Your father and I never held you back."

# Jones Generations

They are members of what the history books refer to as The Silent Generation. Robert and Roberta, born in the 1940s, were both infants during a time of war and melancholy. Grave, disciplined, conventional, and patriotic are characteristics of this generation known to be instrumental in shaping the economic and military power of the United States.

Robert grew up poor, his father sent to prison for check forgery, while his mother worked as a bartender to support him and his younger sister. He picked rocks in farmers' fields to earn money, walked to school in beat-up shoes, and had the reputation of being an all-around tough kid. Options were limited, and after high school he moved to St. Paul to attend barber school.

Roberta was the second, born into what would eventually become a family of nine children. Her father, who was unrecognizable to her when he returned from World War II, worked as a bricklayer, while her mother stayed home and raised the children. Roberta graduated from high school at seventeen and, unsure of what to do next, moved to Minneapolis and worked at a downtown bank. Somewhat of a Mary Tyler Moore figure, she wore long free-flowing dresses and clicked down Hennepin Avenue in high heels.

Eventually Robert — referred to as Bob — met Roberta, married in 1965, and bought a small 1950s-era yellow, three-story home bearing the numbers 208 for $18,500. Bob opened his own barbershop in 1968 and has continued to stand, scissors in hand, behind a chair to earn a living. Roberta raised the kids and cooked the meals, at one time owned a cooking store and then went on to work as a lunch-lady-turned-secretary-turned-business-administrator in the Austin Catholic Schools system.

Born in the 1970s, Casey and Jennifer, along with an estimated forty-four to fifty million other Americans, fall into the category known as Generation X. Characteristics common to this generation include being independent, self-sufficient, and of the mindset of work-to-live versus live-to-work. Casey and Jennifer, along with roughly 60 percent of Generation X, attended college on student loans, worked odd jobs at red-eye hours, landed careers, and later started their own families.

Samantha—born in the 1980s—falls somewhere within the Generation Y category. Known as the Millennial Generation, defining characteristics include being plugged-in twenty-four hours per day and seven days per week, willing to trade high pay for fewer billable hours, achievement oriented, team oriented, and attention craving.

How does Samantha measure up to these standards? She develops a nervous twitch when separated from her Blackberry or Vaio for more than eight hours; the only time her bank account has available funds is when leftover student loan money is deposited; she feels she CANNOT screw up and MUST finish her master's because if she fails to, her mother will disown her since said mother lives vicariously through youngest child; Samantha realizes there is no "I" in "team," and her brother and sister often refer to her as The Golden Child (which she sometimes signs in their birthday cards).

# Feasting on Concrete

At our first Fresh Meat practice at Skateland the trainers tell us that over the next six weeks before Season II starts and league practices begin, our Fresh Meat practices will focus solely on Basic Skills.* These Basic Skills will cover everything from skating in proper derby stance to understanding the rules of the sport. They also tell us that, with the addition of two new home teams making their debut this season, it is essential we newbies get drafted onto home teams as soon as possible and, in order to do that, we have to pass our Basic Skills as soon as possible.

The trainers also mention that during weekday mornings and afternoons FMDG skaters will have open access to the skating surface at the Urban Plains Center (the same place where Coach Mahony's boot camp was held). If we want to go brush up on our skills, all we need to do is fill out a waiver in the UPC office.

I spend my first night of practice trying to learn how to t-stop. To my great surprise, the trainers tell us that NEVER EVER under any circumstances are we to drag our toes to stop. *How stupid*, I think, *a toe stop can't even be used to stop? Why even bother combining the word "toe" with the word "stop" if we can't even use the two together?* One of the trainers must notice the look of confusion on my face so she goes into further detail.

"A toe on the ground equals an unstable ankle in the air," the blonde-haired trainer says, slowly demonstrating the action with her skate, "and an ankle dragging behind a skater who's in the middle of the pack could trip another skater and before you know it — *SNAP* — your ankle is busted like a number two pencil."

On that gory note, I decide it's in my best interest to learn the t-stop. Considered to be one of the very basic stops in roller derby, the t-stop itself involves lining up the inside of one foot directly behind the opposite foot's heel (like a 90-degree angle) and using the back foot's wheels to stop. So, when done correctly, the position of your feet resembles an upside-down T.

The trainers make it look easy, twisting their back foot and coming to a controlled and gentle stop on the track. I, on the other hand, can't perform the basic stop to save my life. My right foot refuses to point east when my left foot is pointed north, and the harder I try the less my right foot wants to bend. And to draw even more attention to my lack of skill, each time I try to stop, the wheels on my right foot make a horrendous *dunk dunk dunk* noise as they bounce up and down trying desperately to grip the floor.

It seems like a majority of the other Fresh Meat skaters grasp the t-stop quickly. I watch them roll across the floor, somehow maneuver their back foot into the correct position, and come to a quiet and controlled stop — just like the trainers.

After a while of waging war against my lead feet, I glance up and notice that a majority of Fresh Meat skaters have migrated to the other side of the track and are being introduced to some other basic stop. *What the Christ?* I think as I realize it's only me and two other skaters still trying to figure out the t-stop. Immediately I realize what's happening — two groups are being formed: the skaters who "get it" and the skaters who "don't get it." *Oh fuck no! I am NOT going to be a member of the shitty skater's club.* In a state of panic, I manage to pull off something that looks somewhat like a t-stop and one of the trainers half-heartedly approves of my effort and sends me down the track to join the "get it" club. I'm safe for the moment but realize I have a lot of work to do.

During my first few weeks on skates, each time I sit trackside to lace up I can almost hear the polished surface growl and snarl in front of me, eager to rip my body to shreds. I fall. A lot. And it hurts. A lot. I feast on concrete and get bruises where bruises shouldn't be. I envy the seasoned skaters who whirl about so fluidly. They appear to have been born wearing skates. They never seem to fall and can execute a stop so fast you can actually smell the burning rubber from their wheels.

Because I want so badly to learn to skate like the seasoned players, each afternoon when I finish cleaning houses I go home, grab a sandwich, change, and hurry off with my derby gear to the UPC arena. Each day I half-heartedly hope to find a few skaters out on the track, taking advantage of the open space and smooth surface, but nobody ever shows. Except for the occasional janitor here and there, I have the entire arena all to myself. I can topple, nose-dive, and roll around on the floor in complete privacy.

When I picture an arena, I think of a loud, busy, rowdy space where one can't even hear herself think. But during my afternoons at the UPC, I can always hear myself think. Hundreds of blue chairs encircling the rink gaze at me in silence, each folded in upon itself, content but at the same time lonely. Each time I adjust my gear, the sound of Velcro from my pads crackles across the rink. When circling around the track practicing crossovers, I hear the clicking of my skates echoing off the hockey boards rhythmically, a metronome keeping pace. And, when I practice falls, the contact between the hard-plated areas of my pads and the concrete floor shatters the silence like a gunshot before fading away into the rafters.

During all my time spent skating alone at the UPC, one afternoon stands out the most. It's the end of August — a hot, humid, sticky day —and I've gotten into the building just as a thunderstorm is about to unleash its wrath. As I sit trackside and gear up, the storm lets loose, and a downpour hammers against the domed roof like thousands of percussionists beating their snares. I'm so distracted by the acoustics and relaxing sounds of the rain and thunder rumbling that I don't even realize I've made my way onto the rink and have been skating the apex of the track performing continuous crossovers around and around. I hadn't fallen when I'd stepped out onto the rink, and I wasn't wobbly. For the first time it seemed like I was actually controlling my skates and directing them where to go. I'd turned my mind off and suddenly the skating was effortless.

# The Red Head

A girl named Rachel started roller derby the same night as I did, but I don't remember much about her from tryouts because I'd been busy shining the floor with my bare knees. At Coach Mahony's boot camp we'd shared an "oh shit" moment when random order in a drill line had paired us together to play defense against three of the league's largest seasoned skaters.

After boot camp I began to realize that this red-haired freckle-faced Rachel girl showed up to every practice from tryouts night on — a true die-hard fan who was as curious and mesmerized by the world of roller derby as I was.

"Henry is the reason I joined roller derby," Rachel says one evening at Skateland as we're gearing up for practice.

Henry is one of the cutest dogs I've seen, a cross between a King Charles Spaniel, a Bichon, and a Jet-Puffed Marshmallow. I'd recently had the pleasure of meeting him one evening when I had stopped by Rachel's downtown apartment.

"Your dog made you join derby?" I ask, tying my skates.

"Pretty much. One day, Henry and I were on the elevator at my apartment because I was taking him out. Then this tattooed girl wheeling around a big suitcase got into the elevator with us. Suddenly, Henry was going nuts humping her leg — this was before I had him fixed — so I screamed and pulled him off her and apologized like crazy. And then I noticed this girl had a helmet attached to her suitcase, so I asked what it was for and she said she played roller derby."

I pause, skate laces still in hand, "So, you're saying if Henry hadn't humped this girl's leg, you wouldn't be skating right now?"

"Mmm hmm," Rachel nods and smiles.

# Survival of the Fittest

Six weeks of learning and practicing Basic Skills serves as a weeding-out process. The falling, hitting, and being hit tests a skater's muscle memory, stamina, and patience. Though twenty skaters had been accepted onto the FMDG league after tryouts, the number of Fresh Meat skaters has dwindled week after week.

One night in particular really tests the character of the newbies. Upon arrival at Skateland, our trainer for the evening — Missy Hit-Her — instructs us not to gear up because we're starting out with off-skates training. We walk onto the track and after Missy welcomes us she says, "Okay ladies, so we're going to start out with an excellent endurance drill [sighs, groaning from the crowd] that I'm sure you all are going to love. We're going to trek down and back across the rink in the army crawl position!"

*Crickets . . . blank stares . . . more crickets.*

Missy lays flat on her stomach and begins to army crawl toward the far end of the rink. She says something about form and transferring weight, but I only hear about 3 percent of her words because I'm 97 percent distracted by her tight gold Derby Skinz* that are being devoured by her Hungry Butt.* With each shift of her leg, the portion of gold spandex covering her butt cheeks dissipates and wanes while the percentage of her fishnets showing steadily increases and waxes. By the time Missy reaches the far end of the rink, her butt has transformed into a fish-netted full moon, which doesn't seem to phase her.

After Missy's demonstration, all of us Fresh Meat skaters lie on the floor and begin the drill on the whistle. Without any knee, elbow, or wrist guards, everyone's bare skin is in direct contact with the polished Skateland track, and upon take-off, the music at the rink is drowned out by skin-squeaking decibels flirting in the ear-bleeding range.

I start the drill next to Rachel, and she and I keep at a steady pace. We're the first to reach the far end of the track. Still lying flat, we each touch the wall, turn around, and start heading back to where we started. The whole time we have both been silent, concentrating on pushing and pulling ourselves across the floor. Three-quarters of the way done, Rachel comes to a dead halt. She turns to me, blows at a dangling piece of strawberry-red hair hanging in her face, and says through gritted teeth, "What does this have to do with ANYTHING!?"

I stop beside her and wrinkle my brow. She poses a good question. What *does* army crawling have to do with roller derby? I haven't seen it anywhere in The Women's Flat Track Derby Association's Basic Skills booklet. Maybe FMDG is secretly affiliated with the army and we're all going through Basic Combat Training without even realizing it? There *is* a skater named Lieutenant Lutefist. And she does have a scary yelling voice, like Sergeant Hartman in *Full Metal Jacket*. What if this Missy Hit-Her trainer is actually Drill Sergeant Hit-Her? Is M16A2 assault rifle training also on the agenda for this evening's practice?

I don't have enough breath to share these thoughts with Rachel, so I answer her question with a groan, and we continue squeaking along.

# Hello, My Name Is

Choosing the right derby name is somewhat of a pivotal step to officially entering into the derby world. Also known as a skater name, a derby name is a nickname used by skaters or officials. Though it isn't required and a few skaters actually skate under their legal name, most derby players choose to go by a different name or alter-ego. Some names are based on puns, others reflect unique characteristics of the skater, and some have nothing to do with absolutely anything at all.

I toy with the idea of going by Large Marge or Tuck N Roll, but upon looking up these names in the international registry of roller derby names (yes, there really is a registry), I see they're already taken.

The birth of my derby name ends up being derived from, of all things, t-shirts. During one of my days spent falling at Coach Mahony's boot camp, I had worn a soccer jersey-like t-shirt with a back side that read *Toni* (short for Luca Toni, the Italian soccer player). The name followed me the rest of the boot camp because apparently *Sammi* is a tough one for people to remember. The second part of my name — Crush — was born on a Friday night when I opened my dresser drawer to discover the only clean article of clothing available for wear was an orange soda-boasting t-shirt.

I like to think I helped Rachel find her derby name. At one practice she had shown up wearing knee-high pink socks that made her legs look like flamingo legs, even more so when we practiced skating on one foot. Thinking I had hit the jackpot of all derby names, I skated up to Rachel and yelled, "Flamingo Hovercraft! That can be your derby name!"

While I thought the name represented creativity at its finest, Rachel found it to be about as attractive as a colonoscopy. She later settled with the name "Dire Fly." At least I had helped her figure out a name she *didn't* want.

# A Brief Text Conversation with Rachel

[Me, Fri. 11:53 p.m.] Watching this sk8board trick thing on ESPN and it's all totally do-able on quad sk8ts. I need 2 learn how 2 do the trix. U can b my safety backup but we won't go 2 the ER.

[Rachel, Sat. 9:27 a.m.] U have cable?

# TURN TWO: THE PACK IS HERE

# Loans

As autumn begins its annual approach, a familiar sense of urgency seems shared by many. Squirrels trade in their lazy summer habits for active winter planning, farmers work late into the night harvesting under the full orange moon, and Mom and I argue incessantly over the phone while scrambling to fill out the FAFSA paperwork I've neglected all summer.

"I don't understand why you always push things off," Mom yells over the phone. "It's not going to be my fault if you don't get your loans and you can't take any classes."

She and I have been filling out FAFSA forms for the past seven (going on eight) years in a row, and every year we have this SAME. EXACT. CONVERSATION. She gets mad at me for dragging my feet, I get mad at her for telling me I drag my feet, she tells me I need to get my act together, and I tell her I learned my act from her. She sighs. I sigh. She swears. I swear.

"What's your financial aid pin number?" she asks.

"I have no idea. You've always kept track of it."

"Samantha Marie, you've got to learn to do this by yourself! I'm not going to be around FOREVER!"

"I *have* tried to do it by myself, but then you always get mad when I do because I don't know what to fill out and not fill out and then you always say 'Oh, just let ME do it!'"

I grit my teeth and squint in anticipation of a snappy comeback, but all I get in return is, "What's your zip code?"

# Tell Me You Washed Your Hands

With the fall semester back in session, Diane agrees to let me keep my cleaning position even though I only have time to work on Fridays. She pairs me up with Marla (a.k.a. the Dust Nazi) who has a tendency to get irked about certain things — streaked wooden floors, the direction of bedroom pillows (the hole part where the pillow is inserted MUST point outward, not inward), and, naturally, dust. Oddly enough, I find her franticness and OCD tendencies to be rather entertaining.

For example, Marla has this funny way of sticking random pieces of fuzz, tiny rocks, and food crumbs into the pockets of her sweatpants. Sometimes, I don't think she's even aware she does it. We'll be getting ready to leave a house and suddenly her eagle eyes will spot a lone Cheerio over in a corner behind a curtain behind a plant that I didn't even know was there. Then she'll run over, being careful to tiptoe across the freshly mopped floor, grab the Cheerio, and stick it in her pocket because we've already emptied all the garbage cans. I sometimes wonder what the bottom of Marla's washing machine looks like.

On a chilly fall morning, Marla and I arrive at one of our usual Friday mid-morning houses. While the house is home to one of my favorite dogs, I'm not a fan of the owners, especially the woman/wife/mother. Each time I've met her she's always come off as a stuck up biznatch who likes to talk down to Marla and me.

I have just finished cleaning the downstairs portion of the house where, once again, the owners had neglected to pick up their kids' toys. Luckily, one of Diane's policies was that her cleaners didn't waste their time picking up other people's shit. If the homeowner didn't have it straightened up, we were to work around it. I'd happily vacuumed in weird streaks around the scattered toys, chuckling to myself because working around the mess cut my vacuuming time in half. I came up from the basement and walked down the hallway toward the master bedroom to find Marla making the bed.

"Done with the downstairs," I say, standing in the entryway to the bedroom. "Like usual, the kids left all their crap out so I just vacuumed around it."

"Did you wipe down the bar tabletop and the barstools?" Marla asks fluffing a pillow.

"Yup, and I dusted off the treadmill too."

"Good," she throws another pillow onto the bed. "Look at what I found in the sheets," she turns around and points at the mantle headboard. "What do you suppose it is?"

Sitting perched atop the headboard is a rubbery, spiky, green, amoeba-looking object.

"Is that . . . ?" I walk into the bedroom for a closer look. I practically choke on my gum as I realize what it is. "Jesus Christ it's a sex toy!" I yell. "Oh God, Marla, please tell me you didn't touch it."

Marla looks at me with wide googly eyes and wrinkles her nose. She looks back toward the frightening object, stares at it for a moment, then walks into the bathroom, pumps the soap dispenser, and cranks the faucet to full blast.

# My Evolutionary Sister

My sister has peculiar cleaning habits. For starters, she doesn't like having any dirty cups or glasses sitting around. And I'm not talking about dirty glasses like *oh-yeah-that-was-last-week's-Sunny D* (likely found at my brother's house); we're talking about glasses that have barely been used. A glass you've maybe just filled with water and haven't even taken a sip from. You walk outside the kitchen, come back five seconds later, and the glass is poof! Gone! Vanished into the dishwasher. The 937 times that I've asked, "Hey, where'd my glass go?" her reply has been, "Oh, that was yours?" There have been times when we've been the only two people in the house for an entire weekend and she's come back with the same "oh, that was yours?" reply. Well who else's glass of ice cube infused water would it be? Because if it's your husband's from thirty-six hours ago when he left to go hunting for the weekend, you sure as shit better patent those Everlasting Ice Cubes before Willy Wonka gets word.

Then there's the vacuuming, which she enjoys too much. The vacuum cleaner she owns is the Lamborghini model of the vacuum world. Named the Evolution, I can't help but call it (fading out toward the end) the EVOlution . . . LUtion . . . lution. When Jen first bought it, she gave me the run-down on the vacuum's specs — the metal handle with soft grip, the easy tool quick draw hose with telescoping wand, the electrostatic hepa media filter — the machine sounded like it was from a different dimension.

Then there's the Rearranging of the Fire Mantle, which may as well be a national holiday in December. Jen likes to have her fire mantle looking in tip-top shape, and she likes to have things on it — candles, a picture, a vase — not too much, not too little. One night I was down visiting for a weekend and we'd just finished setting up the Christmas tree. I came upstairs from watching a movie and went to get something in the kitchen. Jen was standing over by the fire mantle decorating it with a few Christmas items — a red candle here, a green one there. I didn't think much of it and went back downstairs to watch the movie. About an hour and a half later after the movie had finished, I came back upstairs to find Jen STILL standing there at the fire mantle arranging the same red and green candles.

"You're still there?" I said stunned, an empty popcorn bowl in my hand.

"Well, I'm not sure I want this up here," she said, waving a candlestick through the air. "Anyway how was the movie?"

"You mean *movies*," I replied, "you've been standing there in the same spot for so long, your husband and I were able to watch all six *Rocky* movies, all *The Godfather* films, and now we're halfway through the *Jurassic Park* trilogy. Oh, and by the way, you missed Christmas."

# Privileges

It's time for me and a handful of other Fresh Meat skaters to test out of Basic Skills. Testing that evening is held at the Southwest arena, a hockey arena that goes ice-free in the summer. The only problem with the space is that it has ZERO air conditioning. Earlier in the day, the temperature in Fargo had been steamier than the Amazon Basin, and now, even though the sun had set, its disappearance over the horizon hadn't cut numbers on the thermometer.

Chawz, a seasoned skater whom I admire for her skills, hip checks, and uber solid knowledge of gear and skates, is head trainer for the evening while Missy Hit-Her is co-trainer. After warm-ups, Chawz calls our group of ten Fresh Meat skaters to the middle of the track.

"All right ladies, most of you are getting pretty close to passing your Basic Skills," Chawz says, clipboard in hand. "In fact, I think the majority of you just have this one remaining portion left to pass. So tonight we're going to work on taking hits and recovering. I asked a few of the Merby dudes to join us this evening, so they're here to help you get a feel for what it's like to get smacked around. A lot of good female derby skaters hit just as hard, or sometimes I think harder than the guys, so this will give you an idea of how it really feels to bout."

Our instructions are to one at a time go out onto the track

and skate around slowly while three seasoned skaters (two Merby guys and either Missy or Chawz) mercilessly hit each one of us continuously. We're not allowed to counter hit or dodge hits. The whole point of the drill is more about testing stamina and recovery rather than balance and agility.

A Fresh Meat skater who goes by Margo-Forehead is the first to step out onto the track. She appears to be a little gun shy and after the one minute of being blasted by hip checks, shoulder checks, and can openers, she slowly rolls off the track toward us, panting heavily and "whewing" under her breath. Her purple "I ♥ Fargo" t-shirt is covered in dark sweat stains.

Margo, being a good seven inches taller and at least sixty pounds heavier than I, looks like death. Naturally, I'm terrified.

A handful of other Fresh Meat skaters huff and puff their way through their one minute of hell. Some go airborne when hit. Others collapse in place, their legs giving out after being squeezed like a jelly sandwich between two Merby guys. One skater lands in such an awkward position someone in our crowd of Fresh Meat skaters bellows, "That's prolly gonna leave a Giner-Shiner!"*

During Rachel's turn, she remains in perfect derby stance — skates shoulder width apart, knees slightly bent, upper body balanced on hips, chest out proud. She takes hit after hit, comes close to falling once but manages to fully recover without going down.

When it's my turn to test, I roll onto the track and shoot a half smile at Chawz and the two Merby guys.

"Are you ready Toni?" Chawz looks me in the eye.

No sooner do I nod than the hits start coming in at all directions. Wham-BAM-hip-ka-pow-shoulder-KA-BOOM, Toni down.

Toni up: Wham Bam, hip check. Pa-boom, left hip check, Ka-pow, right hip check. KA-BOOM, Toni down.

This Batman comic strip continues on repeat for what feels

like hours. With each blow to my body I "oof" and "poof" louder and hit the ground with less control. My legs burn, my head spins, I'm not sure which direction is derby direction. I get up, I get hit, I fall down. Up. Hit. Down. Up. Hit. Down. Up. Hit. TWEET — Missy's whistle blows when I'm in mid-air. Down.

That evening, all ten of us Fresh Meat skaters pass our Basic Skills.

# Beefy Possibilities

Passing Basic Skills opens a new door into the world of FMDG. For starters, I'm no longer Fresh Meat but rather Tenderized Meat.* I'm also considered an actual member of the league. Rachel, a handful of other freshly tenderized skaters, and I are immediately put into the home team draft pool where, within a few weeks, we will find out which home team we're selected to be on.

The Fargo Moorhead Derby Girls league had steadily been growing in numbers since its initial debut last year in 2009. Home to three universities and a population of people who yearned to see something new, the Fargo-Moorhead area had eagerly embraced the sport of derby and the characters who went with it. Charred Coating — notorious for wearing a wig beneath her helmet and throwing hits like a linebacker — was a fan favorite. Dine'n'Dash was a standout jammer (point scorer) who never ceased to please the crowd with her graceful transitions. A since-banned skater had at one point even given the crowd a taste of old-school derby by tackling a ref during a home team bout.

Our group of skaters is the largest group of newbies the league has ever seen. Between the rising numbers and the positive outcome of season one, a handful of new possibilities including a warehouse, more home teams, and a B travel team present themselves before the start of season two.

# Drafted

I wind up getting drafted to the home team I'd hoped to be on—the Fighting Suzies. One of the original home teams of FMDG, the Fighting Suzies had won last year's championship against the Monkey Wenches and was projected to be one of the favored teams for a repeat win. Because of the drastic increase in the number of skaters (the league was now composed of roughly sixty skaters), two additional home teams had been added to the league: the Haute Dishes and Battlescar Galactica. Rachel winds up getting drafted to the Battlescars.

I've already semi-met two of the more experienced skaters on the Suzies: Dine'n'Dash and Twizzle. At Coach Mahony's boot camp I'd exchanged some witty remarks with the two of them, who were equally sarcastic, and Twizzle had decided to dub me Smart Ass. Charred Coating—who went by Char (pronounced like the *char* in *charcoal*)—is also a member of the Suzies, and I'm especially stoked we're on the same team since any hit I had ever received from Char had always sent me airborne.

An interesting fact about my new team is that, by random chance, it contains the majority of the league's lesbians. Something about this fact feels like a security blanket and perhaps a step in the right direction toward learning to fully embrace my own sexuality.

Though I've never actually come out to anyone, I've always

known that I favor women over men. I had dated a handful of guys who had all been sweet and charming, but whenever one of them flipped the romance switch I always found myself feeling detached and turned off, like an unplugged vending machine. Then this unplugged feeling usually led to flashbacks of junior high science class and our teacher informing everyone that a human's strongest desire (behind survival) was to reproduce. Then on top of all that thinking, I'd ponder my own existence and wonder if my second strongest desire was out of order. It wasn't that I didn't want sex, I just wanted it with someone who didn't have a penis. Was wanting to have penis-free sex an underlying sign that I didn't want to reproduce?

# Derby and Sexual Orientation

Roller derby relies heavily on touch and feel. After all, it's a full contact sport that thrives on close contact with teammates. In order to keep the opposing team's jammer from scoring points, you essentially wall up with your fellow teammates to create a barrier hard for a jammer to break through. Sometimes, while trying to hold back the opposing blocker, you accidently grab your teammate's boob, or her ass, or her crotch. Other times you get so close to a skater's face you practically make out. Sometimes you get tackled, fondled, mounted, and tangled up with a skater in such a way you're certain she's impregnated you.

Just because roller derby requires full physical contact doesn't always mean the skaters themselves are all women who are sexually attracted to other women. When you think of a group of men tackling and beating each other up within the confines of a hundred-yard field, do you assume they're all a bunch of gay men? Guys beat up on other guys in the world of sports and nobody really gives it a second thought. But when women beat up on other women in the world of sports, why does the close contact draw so much attention toward the sexual orientation of the female athlete?

According to Char's partner, a hard-core feminist named Marble-less Mable, "People automatically associate powerful women with butch-like tendencies out of ignorance, fear, jealousy, or all of the above."

# The Yahoo Group

Since being drafted and officially becoming a part of FMDG, my school email account is constantly bombarded by roller derby messages. Whenever I open my inbox with the intentions of downloading the latest class assignment for school or sending out a new story for my writing buddies to critique, I'm distracted by the overabundance of two-word email responses I find in regard to derby.

The Yahoo Group is the main communication portal for FMDG. Each active member of the league is added to the group where practice information, agendas, and league information is shared quickly and easily by the touch of button. The main FMDG group is linked directly to each skater's personal email account so with the click of the send button roughly sixty members receive an instant message.

I've only been a member on the group for a few weeks, but I've already come to the conclusion that, while the Yahoo Group is a great business communication tool, it's also somewhat of a useless chatter and/or bitching zone. Sure, I like to receive emails. And yeah, it's great to have my phone synced to my email account. What gets a tidbit annoying, however, is when, within the matter of a single class period (sixty minutes), I get out of class to find I have eighteen unread emails. *Yay!* I think to myself, *somebody loves me and wants to share information with me!* Or I think, *Gee, eighteen emails within an hour? . . . something important must be happening.* By the time I open each of these eighteen separate emails, I have a total of nine that read, "Yes!" five that read, "No!" three that read, "I don't understand!" and one that reads _____ (because it is blank). After I finally thread back through all of the emails upon emails, I come to find out that each separate response is in reply to one initial message that read, "FYI, we're having practice from 7 to 9 p.m. on Thursday instead of 8 to 10 p.m. Also, bring shoes for off-skates."

# Ages

Sometimes it bothers me that my parents are unusually old for my age. In a way, I guess maybe that sounds sort of ignorant — using my own age to determine whether someone is old. The truth is, I'm twenty-five, about to be twenty-six in a few weeks, and that puts Mom and Dad at sixty-five and sixty-six. For parents, those ages are perfectly normal if you're thirty-nine and forty — the ages of my sister and brother.

In grade school I dreaded those conversations in the lunch room that revolved around how old your parents were. I was a shy kid growing up and wanted nothing more than to eat my bologna sandwich and half listen to the lunchroom chatter. But no, whenever this conversation topic came up — and it did EVERY SINGLE YEAR — no matter how quiet and invisible I wanted to be, some jerk kid always asked loud enough for the whole table to hear, "Hey Sammi, how old are *your* parents?" Never wanting to be a complete outcast and odd ball, since everyone else's moms and dads were in their thirties, and, taking into consideration that most of my friends knew I had an older brother and older sister who were both in college, I'd casually reply "forty-one and forty-two" when, in fact, they were pushing or already well into their fifties. Mom and Dad remained forty-one and forty-two throughout my grade school and junior high years. To my great relief, nobody ever did the math to figure my parents would've been around fifteen when they had my brother. Good thing I didn't hang around the math nerds.

I've spent countless hours throughout my existence wondering if my birth was a complete and utter accident. It *would* explain the large age difference between my siblings and me. It would also explain the excessive coddling I've received (and continue to receive) from my parents, especially Mom. Maybe deep down Mom and Dad truly do know that I was an accident, though they've never actually admitted it, and therefore they've gone to countless and over-the-top measures to make me feel like I really *wasn't* an accident. It would explain the trips to Disney World, new toys, sports equipment, golf lessons, tennis lessons, help with college tuition, new cars, therapy, and cell phone payments. It would also explain the extra money in my checking account, help toward paying medical bills, car payments, and health insurance. And that trip to Key Largo where we went parasailing and snorkeling and deep sea fishing, the steak dinners when I came home to visit, the father/daughter trip to Vegas — maybe the reason behind all of these things is because Mom and Dad felt bad that I was an *oops* so they wanted to cover it up by making sure I didn't feel like an *oops*.

Or maybe there's some other dark underlying secret they're not telling me. Maybe my parents aren't *really* my parents. Maybe I was actually adopted. Maybe my true parents are just some random bums who drank a lot of beer and one night had too much fun after a Springsteen concert. Drunks would explain my drinking habits. Springsteen would explain why I've seen him in concert a few times. And — just like the album — I was "Born in the U.S.A." in 1984.

# Another Brief Text Conversation with Rachel

[Rachel, Mon. 10:55 p.m.] Is it un-feminist to call someone a douchebag? Should we be calling people scrotum sacks or something like that?

[Me, Mon. 11:07 p.m.] Hmm. I never thought about that. Are there more derogatory words that stem from the female side of things?

[Rachel, Mon. 11:09 p.m.] You should probably ask Char's Marble-less Mable.

# Travel Teams

The Women's Flat Track Derby Association is comparable to the National Basketball Association or the National Football League. It is the head governing body of roller derby that is made up of hundreds of teams from the United States and around the world. Through WFTDA sanctioned bouts, travel teams are able to get ranked in the system and thus move up or down in rankings. At the end of a regular WFTDA calendar year, a travel team's ranking determines whether they are eligible to play in regional championships that ultimately lead to another championship that eventually determines the best team in the world.

Due to the exploding growth of the league over the summer, FMDG is now able to support two travel teams — an A and a B. Since FMDG's birth, the travel team had originally been known as the All Stars and had consisted of a handful of league skaters who were willing to travel around the area to play against other teams. Essentially, if you had passed Basic Skills and knew how to tie your skates, you were good as gold to land a spot on the All Stars. But this year, travel team was about to become a team you had to try out for.

It never once crosses my mind not to try out for a spot on the travel team. The sport already has me wrapped around its little wheel. I love the skating, the hitting, the skaters, and I even appreciate the stinky funk of derby gear that radiates off skaters the way garbage radiates out of a dumpster on a muggy summer afternoon. I had recently dropped $300 on new derby skates and intended to get every nickel's worth out of them, and then some. I want to be a good skater. I want to learn how to be that jammer who can score twenty-five points in a single jam. I want to learn how to lay a can opener directly on someone's sternum to send their skates flying out from under them. I want to play roller derby with the big girls.

So I try out for the travel team and land a spot on the B team known as the Fargo Furies (not furries like those people who've channeled their inner raccoon, but Furies like the female spirits in Greek mythology who punished their victims by driving them bonkers). At first, I'm not stoked about being drafted to the B team. Having played numerous sports growing up, I had spent most of my time playing on A teams. In my eyes, a player on a B team wasn't exactly the cream of the crop. But, after attending a few nights of travel team practice, I warm up to the idea that B team is an okay starting point for me. For starters, most A- and B-team practices are combined, so I have the opportunity to play with and learn from the best skaters in the league. Travel team play is also year-round, so I have an ample amount of time to improve and work on my skills. And as an additional perk, Rachel had also made the B team.

# Derby Wife

The sport of roller derby is full of mysterious jargon, quirks, and rites of passage. You wear "panties" on your head, you line up Ass to Vag on the opposing team's blockers, and maybe, a little while into your derby career, you find a derby wife. While not all leagues are into derby wives, FMDG happens to be, and there are a wide variety of happily "married" couples in the league.

What exactly *is* a derby wife? From my point of view, it's a way of branding your closest derby friend as being yours. It's a polite way to say *hands off bitch, she's mine*. Derby spouses come in all varieties and impact the derby "marriage" as a whole. One derby-wife-married-to-a-man plus other-derby-wife-with-kids-and-divorced equals let's hang out and chat over beers at the bar. Or one flaming-homosexual-derby-wife plus bi-curious-derby-wife equals derby wives with benefits.

It's a cold November night in Bemidji and I'm in a downtown bar at an after party. Earlier in the evening I'd skated in a pre-Thanksgiving themed mixer (the Turkeys versus the Cranberries) that consisted of various skaters from around the area.

There's a large crowd in the bar since the mixer bout had been followed by FMDG's travel team, the Northern Pains v. Bemidji's Babe City Rollers travel team. Skaters from Bemidji and FMDG mingle, drink, and peruse around the dance floor.

Rachel and I have been glued at the hip all night. We sit in a booth chatting. She sips from her vodka cranberry and I chug a Miller Lite. As we delve into our own little world, various FMDG skaters stop by our booth to chat. The derby wives come and go: Miracle and Tool Pelt, Missy and Chawz, Twizzle and Dine'n'Dash.

As the night wears on somebody brings up the suggestion that Dire Fly (a.k.a. Rachel) and I should be derby wives. News of this idea travels through the bar and suddenly FMDG skaters are coming over to me saying it must be done, Toni and Fly must get married. Someone hands me the flimsy plastic lid to a condiment cup that once held a Tequila Pudding Shot.* They tell me to use this token as the ring.

I laugh at the whole ordeal because I am the least smooth person on the planet. What if Rachel doesn't want to be my derby wife? What if I propose and get shot down in front of the whole bar? But then, before I can think another thought, somebody grabs my arm and brings me up onto the bar stage. A band isn't playing that night so the stage is empty. I look out at my derby league mates and smile sheepishly as Rachel walks up onto the stage. I'm smirking and laughing, and Rachel is standing in front of me smiling with her lips and her blue eyes.

I get down on one knee and the bar crowd, which has been completely overrun by derby skaters, hoots and hollers. "Rachel, ah I mean Fly," I hold up the plastic lid, "will you be my derby wife?"

"Of course!" she pounces on me and I fall onto my back. I lay on the stage floor, Rachel looking down at me, the crowd clapping and laughing.

"I thought you'd never ask," she says.

# A Sonnet for My Derby Wife

For standing with the suitcase in her hand
your small white fluffy dog did seize his chance
oh Henry NO! you cried out in demand
too late, he's going at it on her pants.

'Tis strange to think the action of a hump
could lead one to a different way of life
for if your dog had not performed the jump
there is no way you'd be my derby wife.

We'd have no Skateland, bruises black and blue
no drifting supermans across the floor
or rink rash, head crash, back bash, twists askew
no tired muscles worn straight to the core.

So cheers to Henry and his horny phase
and long live derby all our married days.

# Pandora's Box*

One day somebody waves a magic wand and POOF the FM Derby Girls have signed the lease to a permanent practice facility. Though I can't recall any meeting that discussed whether signing a three-year, four-grand-a-month contract would be a good idea, it happened anyway.

Eager chatter of "We'll be able to skate whenever we want!" and "FMDG will have a permanent home!" is all anyone seems to talk about at practice, which has still been taking place at Skateland and the Urban Plains Center. Even a database gets set up on the Yahoo Group to collect ideas on what we should officially call the new practice space. (Hands-down winner in my book: "The Church of Skatin'," coined by Char.)

But, as time passes by, the yays and hoorays morph into boos, hisses and "when in the flying fuck are we going to get into the goddamn building?" It turns out the landlord, Mario, functions at the speed of a melting glacier in Antarctica (pre-global warming). The building, which used to be a used car dealership, is practically condemned and not even up to code on city standards.

One afternoon, I have the pleasure of accompanying a few board members to the warehouse to see how things are progressing. The building, located on the older industrial side of Fargo, is quite the looker — peeling paint, walls stained with streaks from rusty roof water, a large plastic sign with cracked and broken letters that spelled out *Auto Repair*. To the north side of the building a parking lot overflows with run-down, rusted-beyond-all-repair cars. It looks like a bleak graveyard for a dealership that must have filed for bankruptcy during Hoover's era.

Beyond two sets of glass doors, up a long staircase, and through another glass door is FMDG's building space. The main entrance  room is carpeted and leads to another carpeted room that will eventually serve as the main gear-up/gear-off area. The air is a stale mix of dust and wet dog. To my best guess, the main culprit to the poor ozone quality lies in the carpet that looks to be harboring some undiscovered bacteria that will undoubtedly — like everything else in the world — lead to lung cancer.

The next room is the main reason for renting out the warehouse — a large, polished, cement-floor area where the main derby track will be laid. The space seems large enough for one track and, most likely, a second half-sized track. The space is well lit with long panels of fluorescent ceiling lights, and there are two windows for some natural lighting. However, there is one slight problem: a large gaping hole in the very center of the floor. The hole is rectangular and completely open — no railings, no side walls — and there's a cement staircase at one end of the rectangle that leads down into the dark bowels of the building. With the illumination from the ceiling lights I look down into the hole to see boxes, tools, Satan and his band of demons betting a fiddle of gold against Johnny's soul, a random golf cart, and a large electrical panel at the very bottom of the steps. Taking everything about the hole into account, it seems likely that a tumble off the ledge or down the stairs will ultimately result in a Fourth of July firework display and a closed casket ceremony.

Near the back of the main track-to-be area, a long row of rusty lockers stands along the wall. At first glance it looks like the perfect place to store stinky pads, skates, and helmets. But after further inspection, I discover the width of each locker to be the size of a Coke can—the perfect place to store a pair of kid-sized skis.

A used-to-be kitchen area is at the back of the warehouse and, beyond that, a scary looking locker room, and beyond that, an even scarier looking bathroom equipped with a dirty shower stall lacking a curtain.

But minus the mold, mildew, potential asbestos, ten years of dirt, and gate to hell, the space is FMDG's and there are some definite positives. FMDG will no longer have to rent out from Skateland or the UPC, which means the league will no longer have to align practice times with the availability of the roller rink or the UPC. If we want to have practice at midnight, we can. We'll also have a place to leave all of our gear. And we'll have a set place for league meetings (rather than having to rent out a room at the coffee shop).

## And Yet Another Brief Text Conversation with Rachel

[Me, Thurs. 3:06 p.m.] Last night I had a dream that zombies were attacking me so I filled a green squirt gun w/ holy water and shot @ them but it had no effect. What do you suppose this means?

[Rachel, Thurs. 4:41 p.m.] You're Catholic.

# TIMEOUT: DERBY 101

**THE GEAR!**

To keep medical bills to a minimum, a skater is required to be equipped with gear that has the ability to sustain high impact falls, slips, collisions, tackles, and any other form of reckless behavior pertinent to the derby world.

High impact helmet

Wig and sunglasses optional

Mouth guard

Elbow pads

Wrist guards

Derby Skinz Oh la la!

Killer 187 knee pads

Wicked cool bruise

Quad skates ( no blades allowed! )

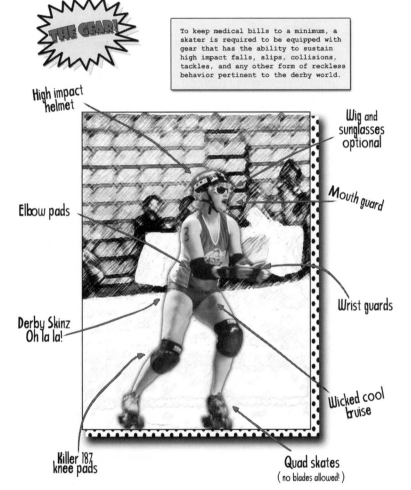

Roller derby is a sport played by two teams of five members. The main objective is to get your team's jammer (the point scorer who wears a star on her helmet) through the pack (the largest group of blockers) as quickly as possible.

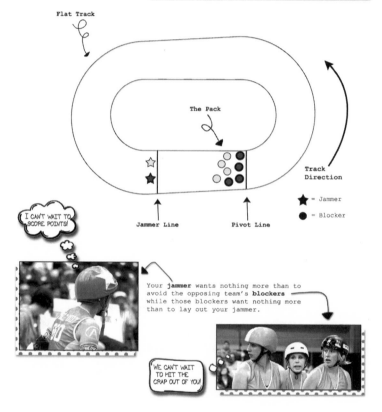

The first jammer to get through the pack (without incurring any penalties) becomes the **lead jammer**.

The jammers continue sprinting around the track trying to catch up to the back of the pack again.

For every opposing blocker a jammer passes, her team scores a point.

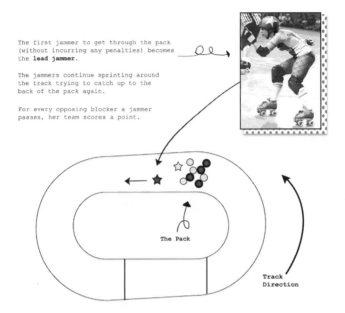

The Pack

Track Direction

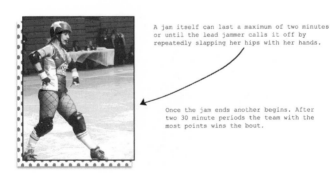

A jam itself can last a maximum of two minutes or until the lead jammer calls it off by repeatedly slapping her hips with her hands.

Once the jam ends another begins. After two 30 minute periods the team with the most points wins the bout.

Sometimes skaters have so much fun playing derby that rules just seem to slip right out of their minds. To stay out of the **penalty box** it's best to:

**Avoid hitting...**
 *the head
 *the back, rear of butt and legs
 *the knees, lower legs

**Avoid hitting with...**
 *elbows
 *forearms/hands
 *the head
 *below mid-thigh

Blocking is any movement on the track
designed to knock the opponent down or out
of bounds or to impede the opponent's speed
or movement through the pack.

Aim for...
  *arms and hands
  *chest/front/side of torso
  *hips
  *mid and upper thigh

Aim with...
  *arm from shoulder to elbow
  *torso
  *hips and booty
  *mid and upper thigh

The Women's Flat Track Derby Association (WFTDA) requires that a skater be able to pass a minimum set of basic skill requirements in order to be eligible to bout.

### 1. Skating Skills

Crossovers    Plow stops

### 2. Falls

### 3. Balance/Agility

### 4. Skating with Others

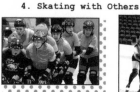 

Pack Skating

Whips

### 5. Blocking

### 6. Rules

What is the referee whistle signal
for a major penalty?
a. No whistle signal
b. Two rapid whistle blasts
c. One long whistle blast
d. Two long whistle blasts

**1935:** Sports promoter Leo Seltzer invents a sport utilizing roller skating participants. His idea—Transcontinental Roller Derby—is an endurance race that features a team of one woman and one man skating the distance of the U.S. (coast to coast) on a banked track.

A QUICK HISTORY!

**Late 1930s:** A New York sportswriter suggests that derby have more rules and more contact between skaters. Leo likes the idea and the sport evolves into a game skated between two teams of five women and five men scoring points by lapping opponents. The new rules also emphasize physical blocking.

**1948:** Derby grabs national attention when televised from the 69th Regiment Armory in New York City.

**Late 1950s-1960s:** Leo transfers derby to his son, Jerry. Soon after, derby takes a theatrical turn for the worst. Skaters become frustrated and  quit.

**1973:** Jerry Seltzer shuts down derby.

**1980s-1990s:** Attempts to bring back the sport are short lived.

**Early 2000s:** The roller derby of today gets its start with the Texas Rollergirls in Austin, Texas.

**2004:** The United Leagues Coalition (ULC) forms and consists of a handful of flat track derby leagues who want to turn roller derby into a modern sport.

**2005:** The ULC holds its first meeting with the goal of developing the guiding principles of the organization. Twenty leagues are represented. The ULC later votes to change its name to the Women's Flat Track Derby Association (WFTDA).

**2010:** There are more than 450 flat track roller derby leagues around the globe.

# TURN THREE: MAJORS

# Little Blue Pill

After a Wednesday evening screenwriting class, Lonny Blossoms walks over to me, backpack in hand, and asks if I'm interested in hitting up the Knights of Columbus for a pitcher or two. Never in my life have I turned down an invitation to go out drinking, so his question poses no contemplation on my end. Lonny tells me he's also going to invite Cronon, a guy new to the grad program.

Besides screenwriting class, Cronon and I also attend the same poetry workshop every week. The analysis I'd gathered on him was that he mostly kept to himself. He always sat in the back of the classroom and often times seemed spaced out and in his own world. However, when he did throw his two cents in during class discussions, his opinions were always interesting.

The three of us hit the pitchers of beer hard that night. We talked about the usual after-class topics — what we liked about the material we'd read before the class and what we thought of the material we'd critiqued for the night.

Around 11:00 p.m. the bartender tells us she's getting ready to close up. It's a weeknight and Lonny, Cronon, and I are the only regulars left. We finish our beers and decide that since we're having such a good time shooting the breeze and getting drunk, we might as well head downtown for a nightcap.

As we walk across the Main Avenue bridge that connects Moorhead, Minnesota, to Fargo, North Dakota, Cronon pulls out a little pill bottle that rattles. "You guys want one?" He shakes the bottle like he's mixing a martini.

"What is it?" I ask curiously. "Just so you know, I don't do drugs, just alcohol."

"It's not illegal, silly," Cronon rolls his eyes, "It's a prescription I take when my anxiety is really bad."

"Sure Cronon, give me one of 'em," Lonny holds out his hand.

"Wait wait wait, what's it do?" I ask.

"It helps you to relax," Cronon replies as he shakes a pill into Lonny's hand. "Like I said, I take it when my anxiety is really bad."

"Oooh, so it's just a relaxer?"

"Yup."

"Ok, gimme one."

*One hour later . . .*

"Croooonon . . . gimme another one of those little blue pills," I say and lean over the table toward him. "I doooon't think it's wooorking."

Lonny laughs and Cronon shakes another pill into my hand.

*The following morning . . .*

I wake up groggy in bed, my head whirling in circles. I have no idea what day it is or why I feel so completely out of it. Normally I don't get hung over anymore. Ever since I started grad school, my body has adapted to running on booze. But for some reason this morning feels different. The harder I try to figure out what happened the night before the less I can remember.

I call Lonny to get a recap of the night.

"Heyyy, Sammi," he says into the phone. "How you doin', kid?"

"Blossoms, what in the Christ did we do last night? I remember being at the Knights of Columbus and walking downtown and then asking Cronon for another one of those pills. Besides that, my mind is completely blank."

Lonny laughs in his high-pitched chuckle, "Wow kid, you really WERE outta it."

This response is never a good one to hear after a blackout night.

"So we each took a little blue pill while walking over to Fargo," Lonny says.

"Yup, I remember that part."

"Then, a little while after we got downtown, Cronon gave you another blue pill."

"Yeah, I remember that too," I say.

"Well after that you were loose as a goose. It was as if you had no control at all over your body. At one point we were sitting up at the bar on one of the stools getting ready to order another shot and you literally toppled over backwards off the chair."

"Holy shit, REALLY?" I yell.

"Yeah, you were out of it. Then one of the bouncers came over and I told him we were already on our way out, since we were about to get kicked out anyway. So we called a cab. Then while standing out front waiting for the cab you fell over into one of the bushes."

I snort a chuckle into the phone.

"So we helped you out of the bushes and when the cab arrived I got in with you and helped you back to your apartment. You don't remember any of this at all?"

I'm silent for a moment, thinking hard and trying to let what Lonny said sink in. "Nope," I finally say, "don't remember a thing."

# Forgive Me Father

Growing up Catholic, I was trained to believe alcohol, tattoos, and piercings were all taboo; sex outside of marriage was a sin; birth control was wrong; abortion was a grave evil; and same-sex intimate relationships were a complete and utter disgrace toward God and the church.

Throughout my years as a Catholic school student, all the way up to the day of my high school graduation, it was stressed by teachers, sisters, and priests over and over again that if one were to participate or engage in any of the aforementioned sins one was most certainly destined to be handed — by Jesus himself — a one-way, non-refundable ticket to hell.

Have I mentioned my ticket collection?

# The Déjà 500*

A Sunday morning league practice makes me wonder, again, if FMDG really is affiliated with the US Army and its basic combat training.

Déjà Who, a skater and league trainer who also happens to be a personal trainer at a local gym, is in charge of practice. After a five-minute warm-up on skates, Déjà calls everyone over to the center of the main track, beside The Box.*

"All right ladies, we need to get things started quickly so we don't run out of time," Déjà says while taking attendance on her clipboard. "Today is going to be all about endurance. I suggest that if your water bottle isn't full, you get it filled now because you won't have any time once we get started."

Déjà finishes attendance, sets the clipboard on The Box, and tells everyone to partner up. Rachel isn't at practice this morning, so I partner with Butternut Squash, a decent skater who's been with the league since it formed.

"So here's how this drill is going to go," Déjà says and skates to the center of the track. "Skater one will start on the pivot line and, upon my whistle, start skating and complete twenty laps."

A few people let out "oofs" when they hear the phrase, "twenty laps."

Déjà continues, "Skater two will stand off the track and count laps for her partner. When skater one completes her twenty laps, she'll skate off the track and tag her partner's hand. Skater two will then skate onto the track and also complete twenty laps. While skater two is on the track, skater one will do twenty pushups quickly so she can count laps for her partner," Déjà looks around to be sure we're following. "Then once skater two has completed her twenty laps, she'll tag skater one who will then go out to skate nineteen laps while her partner does twenty pushups. To keep it simple, the number of laps you do will also be the number of pushups you do. And on a side note, if I see any Flo-Hos* out there on the track, everyone is going to do extra pushups."

I look at Butternut Squash because it suddenly occurs to me where this drill is going.

"Skaters one and two will continue switching on and off. Nineteen laps, nineteen pushups, eighteen laps, pushups, seventeen, sixteen, fifteen . . . all the way down to one lap"; Déjà holds up her pointer figure for added effect.

By now everyone is exchanging nervous glances and realizing that when Déjà said endurance she really meant endurance.

A random skater shouts out, "That's like two-hundred-ten laps PER PERSON!"

Déjà smiles and nods. "Which equals out to be just under eight miles for each skater."

# Bald

It's a cold November evening, and I'm out having drinks with my friend Daman (pronounced *Dah-Mahn*). I like hanging out with him because he's crazy-smart, knows how to carry on a good conversation, and has a unique accent that's easy on the ears. He's originally from India and currently in the United States on a student visa attending school at North Dakota State University for some PhD program in engineering or biochemistry or something smart like that.

A few drinks into the night, we somehow get onto the topic of short hair.

"Jeeze, I'd sure love to just shave my head," I say. "I mean, I know it's already pretty short right now," I rub my hand through the three inches on top, "but I've always been jealous of guys because they can shave their head. Why can't a woman shave her head?"

"Well," Daman says in his Indian accent that makes everything sound dainty yet matter of fact, "my pareents sent me an early holiday gift that conetains hair gel, sceesors, a rayzer, and a buzz-er. I have not even used any of the prodicts yet. We could shayve your head tonight if you wanted to."

"Wait a minute," I chuckle and lean over my beer, closer to Daman. "Why would your parents send you a *haircut* kit?"

"Becoz many men in my country keep their hair very short. It is somewhat of a tradeeshon."

"Interesting," I nod. "So what you're saying is that you'd shave my head for me if I wanted it shaved?"

"Ouf course," he smiles.

"Let's get more beer and I'll think about it."

*Later that night . . .*

"Shorter," I say. Looking in the mirror at my buzzed head my scalp is surprisingly white. I take another sip from the can of Bud Light Daman offered me when we'd arrived at his house.

"Shorter?" he turns off the buzzer.

"Yes, definitely shorter. If I'm going to shave my head, then I'm going to shave my head ALL. THE. WAY."

I take a seat on the edge of Daman's bathtub and close my eyes as he lathers what's left of my hair with men's Gillette. Daman's hand rests on the side of my cheek and I feel the cold tip of the razor work its way from my forehead to the back of my neck, the last minuscule strands of my hair crackle as the triple blade razor cuts through them.

After a few minutes Daman announces he's finished and clanks his beer can against mine in celebration.

I shake the towel away from my neck. Small bits of light brown hair sprinkle onto the floor. Turning toward the mirror, I'm shocked by the sheer whiteness of my bald head. Somehow it's whiter than my face, which I didn't know was possible. In fact, my head is so white that it brings to mind the word *albino*, which then makes me think of meteorology class during my undergrad in which we discussed the term *albedo*, meaning the amount of light a surface object reflects. Basically, the albinoness of my head would have an albedo factor similar to that of fresh snow. Breaking it down even further, if I were to step outside without a hat into broad daylight, the astronauts aboard the ISS would be calling down to Houston asking for intelligence on the bright light radiating from the middle of North America. I turn my head to one side and look in the mirror. Turn my head the other way, look. Then turn around and glance over my shoulder to see the back of my head.

"Can you see the big bump on the back of my head?" I rub my fingers across it.

Daman looks closer. "What bump?"

"One that's been there since forever," I grab Daman's hand and move his fingers over the spot. "I sometimes think I was dropped on my head when I was little and my parents never told me."

One thing about being bald in November is that it's flipping cold. The whole deal about a large quantity of heat escaping from your head is no joke, and for the first few weeks of my baldness I go to bed every night wearing a blanket around my head, wrapped up like Miss Cleo.

Most of my derby friends are thrilled to see my new haircut, especially Femme, a gender studies grad student attending one of the universities in town. She tells me my new look is empowering to women, which makes me blush because I have a bit of a crush on her.

When I next see Lonny Blossoms on campus, he is especially enthralled with my bald head and starts referring to me as Sinead. The rest of my grad studies friends also approve of my new look.

The only person I'm nervous to show my haircut to is Mom. It sounds ridiculous that a twenty-six-year-old woman is nervous to show her mother a new haircut, but the relationship between my hair and Mom had a history.

Growing up, I had long blonde hair that extended down to my butt and was thicker than a horse's mane. Mom loved that she could French braid it, curl it for Sunday church, and put it into darling pigtails or ponytails. I hated it with a passion. It took hours to dry, was a snarled mess in the mornings, and, while in a ponytail, was a nuisance when trying to wear a fitted baseball cap.

One day in first grade, my friend Karl Gershwin showed up to school sporting a new haircut with his initials — KG — buzzed into the back of his head. The sheer awesomeness of the spectacle had caused my jaw to hit the playground blacktop, and for the rest of the school day I was tortured by those perfectly outlined letters on the back of Karl's head because he sat at the desk directly in front of me.

That evening after school I informed Mom that it was time I get a real haircut. She tried to talk me into just a trim or a couple of inches off, but I was adamant that it needed to be a real haircut. After numerous attempts of trying to talk me out of a real haircut, Mom finally threw in the towel declaring, "I'm sick of the stubbornness you've inherited from your father." While I wasn't able to get my initials buzzed into the back of my head, I did get my hair reduced from butt-length to chin-length. On a side note, Mom kept the original braid the hairdresser had cut the day of my real haircut. I found it odd at the time that someone would want to keep a lock of hair. I find it odd that, twenty-plus years later, she still has that lock of hair.

The first time Mom sees me with a bald head she nearly screams in horror. It's Thanksgiving and I've just arrived at my brother's house. It's cold outside, so I'm bundled up in all things winter, including a stocking hat. My brother and his wife have four kids who are all under the age of ten, so, as usual, the environment is a mix of chaos and more chaos. I walk in through the door and my nieces run yelling, "Sammi's here! Sammi's here!" which makes me feel like a celebrity. Mom is in the kitchen with my sister-in-law helping prepare the stuffing, turkey, mashed potatoes, sweet potatoes, gravy, pumpkin pie, and apple pie — the classic over-the-edge American meal that could feed a small country for weeks.

As I wave to everyone yelling their "hellos," I see Mom moving toward me to dish out her usual welcome hug. Suddenly time slows down and the action of Mom drawing closer to me is in slow motion. My stomach is in knots knowing that what I'm about to show her could quite possibly ruin her entire existence. *Oh God, Mom's going to kill me. I'm going to die. Don't take your hat off, stupid!*

Somehow my arm deceives me, slowly moving upwards, my hand reaching toward my hat. Mom draws closer and closer, her voice deep and slow saying, "Helllllo sweeeeetie," arms extended in a hug.

And, with a grab of the hand, the hat goes flying off my head.

Mom freezes with her arms still outstretched. Her eyes bulging like an owl's.

"Samantha Marie!" she yells, a quiver in her voice as her arms drop to her sides, a spatula still in hand.

My family members "ooh" and "ahh" and I hear my brother chuckle as he leaves the kitchen and heads toward the family room.

When I glance back at Mom, our eyes lock and for a split second hers appear watery. She extends her arms again, embraces me in a half hug, then turns back toward the kitchen.

# Reality

Reality doesn't exist in a bar. That's why going to the bar is so much fun, because none of it is real. It's a grown-up's playground. People who live in a bar never grow up. They never face reality. Everything is make-believe. The unreal makes the real more tolerable. A bar is like a turtle shell. When outside of it you're exposed to everything life. But inside the shell, everything life is cozy and warm and the beer never runs out. In a bar, reality hangs high above your head. The more you drink the higher it rises. But then you walk out the door and it all comes crashing back down. The more you drink the harder reality falls from the sky. Sometimes I send my reality so high that when I step out the door the effect of its weight crashing down on me is so great that it causes me to pass out in a snow bank. Or a bush; or a dark alley; a random yard. A church entryway.

# Dire Confessions

One evening, while out for beers with Rachel and her roommate Arizona (a.k.a. Number Muncher who takes stats at our bouts) our conversation topic shifts to crappy things that have happened to us. Our competitive natures kick in and suddenly we're each trying to outdo one another with ridiculously random eye-opening whopper stories.

Arizona: *When I was sixteen and living in California, my mom got really drunk one night and decided she needed to see her friend in Colorado. I told her she couldn't drive because she was too drunk and insisted it was silly because my little brother and I had school the next day. But when she told me I could keep the house and live there by myself, I took the keys from her, got my little brother and mom into the car, and took off for Colorado in the middle of the night. After a few hours of driving, my mom woke up from her passed out slumber in the passenger seat and decided Colorado was too far of a drive and it was time to go home.*

Me: *A few years back, during my undergrad, I went through a dark period that consisted of depression, anorexia, and a general hatred toward myself. Because I couldn't ever sleep, I usually got up early in the morning to go for a run—not because I needed the exercise, but because I was trying to run away from myself. Anyhow, during one run I knew something was wrong about halfway through. I started seeing little black spots, my chest cramped up, and I had to lie down on some random person's front lawn. Luckily, the neighbors weren't awake to see me sprawled out in their yard. Not my best moment.*

Arizona and I turn to Rachel who is downing her glass of wine and looking somewhat distraught.

Rachel: *Okay, so I went through a really down-and-out time during my undergrad years as well. I was sad, hated school, hated my life, the usual things. Anyway, spring break rolled around and my sister came down to pick me up at school and give me a ride home. While she and I are driving home, she says as casual as could be, "Oh, by the way, Grandma died a couple weeks ago." Naturally I yelled "What!" and started to cry. I didn't really know what to say because I was really close to my grandma and now suddenly she was gone. Then my sister went on to say, "Yeah, we already had the wake and buried her." I asked why she and my parents didn't tell me. Her response was, "Well, we knew you were having a hard time and we didn't want to upset you any more than you already were."*

Traumatic Experience Tally Board:

      Arizona:  0

      Me:       0

      Rachel:   1

# Protocol

If FMDG were to schedule a travel team bout (A or B) in Canada, it would be a generous guesstimate that roughly 25 percent of the travel team skaters wouldn't be allowed to so much as sneeze on Canadian soil. Canada gets all up in arms about DUI offenses in the United States and wants you to feel bad about your pour mistake by banning you from the country for at least seven years.

While I'm currently not on Canada's no-go list (as far as I know), I came pretty close a year before I joined derby.

June 2009: It's Friday night and I'm ready for an evening out on the town. Steve, a blonde-haired, blue-eyed architect I'm semi-dating is a guitarist in a band that is slated to perform at a local bar. On my way downtown, I swing by the bank to hit up the ATM machine and when I hit the forty dollars cash option button an annoying beeping sounds and is followed by a flashing message that reads: *INSUFFICIENT FUNDS*. [Okay somebody hit the pause button for a second. In a perfect world any sane and responsible person with half a brain would have stopped to contemplate, *Hmmmm, I don't seem to have the money to go out tonight; therefore, I probably shouldn't go out tonight. Oh and drinking is really bad for my health anyway. I'm probably better off heading back home and watching a movie.* But no, I had to be that irresponsible half-brained person who couldn't rationalize not getting shit-faced on a Friday night. Okay, unpause]. This message is nothing new. I grumble and hit "Continue Transaction" even though I know I'll get charged with an overdraft fee.

I start drinking somewhere around 7:30 p.m. while watching Steve and his band perform. Around ten o'clock, when the band is done, Steve decides he's tired from working all week and heads home while I drive over to another bar to meet up with some friends.

As the night wears on, I continue to drink. My drinking nights are always the same: get downtown early and start off with light beer, then, around midnight, start adding in the hard stuff—a shot here or there, then vodka cranberry the rest of the night.

Around 2:00 a.m., my friend Tara and her friend Lance decide to head over to Tara's apartment a few blocks north of the bar scene.

"Do you think we should call a cab?" Tara asks as we semi-stumble down the steps of the bar's entrance.

"Naaah," I pull out my keys. "I parked in the lot across the street. I ain't walking anywhere."

"Are you sure you should be driving?" Tara looks at me.

"Pfshh, I'm totally fine to drive."

I scan the parking lot as I start my car and, with no cops in sight, I drive out of the lot and head north on Broadway.

"Okay, you have to remind me where to turn," I say.

Tara replies, "15th Avenue North."

"Um, that doesn't help cuz I can't see the signs. Just tell me when to turn."

"Okay, turn now!"

I slam on the brakes and veer left.

"Whoa, I didn't know it was that close!" I straighten out the wheel, step on the accelerator, and turn around to smile at Lance in the back seat.

"WATCH OUT!" Tara screams.

BAM! My seat belt tightens around my chest and my head flings back then forward toward the steering wheel.

Silence.

"Holy shit," somebody mutters.

A random dog starts barking.

"HOLY FUCK!" I look up to see a Ford truck directly in front of my car. The truck's front left bumper is slightly warped and dented.

I throw my door open and scramble around to the front of my car. The left side of my Chevy is twisted and mangled, the bumper sprawled out on the road.

Tara and Lance run over next to me, both wide-eyed and swearing.

"Let's get the bumper into the backseat," Lance whispers while scoping the dark neighborhood to see if anyone is watching. The neighborhood dog continues to bark as Lance and I shove my mangled front bumper into the backseat.

I turn back around toward the Ford and stare at the glass covering the street.

"Come on!" Lance yells from the backseat of my car. He's snuggled up against the bumper and Tara is already back in the passenger seat.

I hop in my car and the engine coughs then manages to start.

"My apartment is right down the block," Tara says. "Let's get the car into the parking lot."

My little Chevy chugs down the block, and I crank the wheel with all my strength just to turn into Tara's parking lot. I drive to the back of the lot, park beneath a light pole projecting a dull orange glow, and kill the engine.

Silence.

Tara and Lance get out of the car and walk around to the front, examining the damage. Tara rubs her nose and I ask if she's all right.

"I lost my nose ring," she says.

Everything seems surreal. *How did this happen? What happened? Oh my God my CAR! Mom and Dad are going to kill me. I'll say somebody hit me, yeah, somebody came out of nowhere and hit me . . . then they left.*

"Come on, let's go inside and lie low for a bit," Tara walks to the entrance of the apartment building. Lance follows her up the two steps to the door and both turn and look at me. As Tara turns the key to unlock the door, a bright beam of light shoots through the darkness and blinds me. Squinting and holding a hand up to my face, I realize it's the cops. I look over to where Tara and Lance are, but they're not there anymore. The front door to Tara's apartment is shut and I'm alone.

"How did you find me anyway?" I ask while handcuffed in the back seat of the SUV.

"We followed your transmission fluid," one of the cops says glancing at me in his rearview mirror.

"Huh." I look out the window at the dark and vacant streets. Low music from the front area of the SUV drifts into my back seat. The cops have left the sliding plastic separator open so we can talk. I don't pose much of a threat, since I'd basically surrendered myself up as soon as they had arrived.

"My parents are going to kill me," I say.

Neither of them comment.

One moment I'm out enjoying a night on the town and getting lit up drunk. The next moment I'm walking the straight line of the transmission fluid from my demolished car.

"Okay, Samantha, walk toward me keeping your head up while placing the heel of one foot onto the front of your other foot," the buzz-haired officer says holding his flashlight in one hand.

*Okay, come on, you can do this. Just walk the line. Sober up, sober up. You've got this.* I start walking. Right foot heel to left foot toe. Left foot heel to right foot toe. I feel like I'm doing an excellent job, but when I shift my eyes to look at the flashlight-in-hand cop, his grimaced expression tells me he's not impressed.

"Samantha, I'm going to have you follow my finger," Officer Buzz says while standing directly in front of me.

*Okay just follow the finger, follow the finger.*

I follow his pointer finger around for a while and then he puts his hand down.

"Did I pass?" I ask.

He answers my question by saying we're moving on to another test where I'm to balance on one foot.

*Pfshht, one foot one shmoot.* Officer Buzz steps back from me, and I raise my right foot off the ground. I waiver for half a millisecond and drop my foot back to the ground.

"Wait, lemme try this foot," I lift my left foot off the ground. *Come on be like one of those goddamn trees they're always talking about in yoga class.* I rock around for half of a half of a millisecond then drop my foot to catch myself from falling.

"For the record," I say to Officer Buzz, "I'm no good at balancing on one leg even when I'm sober."

"Samantha, I'm going to read you your rights," the passenger-side cop says as he handcuffs me and helps me into the backseat of the Fargo Police SUV.

I pay no attention to what the passenger cop is saying because I've heard it too many times in the movies. When he finishes telling me my rights, we're on the way to the ER because I've agreed to have my blood drawn for a blood-alcohol test. Neither of the cops had offered me a breathalyzer, but rather asked if I was willing to submit to a blood test. Somewhere, stuffed way in the back of my memory, I remembered it was always in the best interest of the arrestee to submit to whatever the cops asked. I figured I might as well give in to the system because I was doomed anyway. I'd smashed up my car, fled the scene of an accident, and miserably failed three sobriety tests.

I stare out the window of the SUV and think about all the times I'd driven around drunk without ever being caught. Numerous days and nights in St. Cloud, dozens of times in Fargo — there were too many to count.

"So, can I get a lawyer?" I ask slightly leaning forward to the plastic divider.

"Yes, you have the right to get a lawyer," Officer Buzz says.

"Do you think I should get one?"

"I can't tell you whether you should or shouldn't get one, Samantha," he replies.

The two of them are nice enough, and even somewhat polite. They both seem to be under the impression that I'm not supposed to be in this sort of environment. I know I'm not supposed to be here. I'm a good person, a decent student, a born-and-raised Catholic. I come from a good family. No one in my family has ever had problems with the law. This is all just one big mistake.

One perk about going to the ER with the cops is that you get premiere service. Never, in all of the times I've been to the ER, have I ever been escorted to the front of the waiting line.

When we arrive at the police station, Officer Buzz helps me from the back of the car. He tells me we have to keep the handcuffs on for now, until we get inside, because it's protocol. He escorts me into the building and I check in at a front desk. By now I really have to pee, but the lady behind the desk says I can go after I get frisked.

Officer Buzz unlocks my handcuffs, and I stand up against a wall to get frisked.

"You won't find anything," I say to the lady as she pats me down.

"I'm sure I won't, Samantha," she replies, "but it's protocol."

When I return to the front desk — after having gone to the bathroom — the lady behind the counter instructs me to have a seat. She tells me my bail is set at $500 and asks if I want to call someone to pick me up.

"I don't see that you're going to be a problem here, Samantha," she says and hands me my cell phone and wallet that had both been taken away during the frisking.

"So I don't have to go in a cell?"

"No, we're not going to bother with that," she says.

I call the only person I can think of who might have enough money to bail me out.

"Hello?" a groggy voice answers.

"Steve?" my voice shakes and my eyes tear up, "I'm in jail." A feeling of guilt suddenly hits my stomach and it's at this instant I know the booze is beginning to wear off.

"What?" he says, his voice clearer.

"I ruined my car and got arrested. Can you come bail me out? It's $500. Cash."

Silence fills my earpiece and after a moment he says, "Yeah, yeah, I'll be right there. Where are you?"

"Um, jail."

"I know, but which one?" he asks.

"There's more than one?"

After relaying the address from the clerk to Steve, I hang up and walk over to the vacant waiting area. My head is throbbing so I take a seat in a stiff-backed orange chair and look up at the TV where Sports Center is on. I decide to call my sister, even though it's 4:30 in the morning.

The phone rings a few times and a tired voice on the other end says, "Mmmm, hello?"

"Jen," I say trying to fight back tears and keep my voice under control.

"Sam?" she says, "What's wrong? What's going on?"

"I'm in jail."

Silence.

"Ooh, nooo," she says drawing out the no.

I hear a muffled voice in the background, and it's my brother-in-law asking what's going on. Jen half covers the mouthpiece of the phone and says, "Sam's in jail."

"What happened?" she asks.

"I dunno. I was drunk and smashed my car." My eyes burn with tears.

"Oh God, are you all right?"

"Yah, I'm fine. Somebody is coming to get me right now. Anyway, I just wanted to call and tell you. I gotta go now, so I'll talk to you later. And please don't tell Mom yet."

"Yeah, call me later today or whenever you can talk."

Steve halfheartedly smiles at me when he walks through the police station's front entrance. I force a half smile and stand up to go. I watch as he forks over the stack of twenty-dollar bills, and I tell him I'll pay back every dollar.

As he drives me to my apartment, I explain a few of the details to Steve. I struggle to talk as my bottom lip quivers. When we pull up to the front of my apartment, Steve says, "Why don't you go in and get some sleep and we'll talk about this in the afternoon." He squeezes my hand, "I'll come over and get you later and have a look at your car. We'll work at getting this squared away."

As Steve and I wait for a tow truck to pick up my car, I'm digging through my glove compartment looking for my auto insurance card when I notice a tiny sparkle of light twinkle from the dashboard. I lean in closer to see a small silver object resting in the crease of the passenger airbag unit that failed to deploy. Picking up the object, I hold it between my thumb and forefinger and delicately twirl it around, examining it from all angles trying to figure out what it is. A week later I will wake up in the middle of the night and realize the mysterious silver object was Tara's nose ring.

## The Grand Totals of a Grand Mistake:

Failure to keep vehicle under control: $30
Money back from totaled car: $2,600
Lawyer's fee: $2,500
Reckless driving fee: $500
Money loaned for bail: $500
3-hour Victim Impact Panel class: $75
6-hour Don't Drink and Drive class: $100

Having your parents and boyfriend bail your twenty-four-year-old ass out . . .
Pricelessly embarrassing.

# Concussion

My recollection of the following subject is similar to Baker Street in London — foggy and mysterious. So, to help fill in the missing pieces, I've included Rachel's perspective because, that evening, she happened to be an NSO (Non-Skating Official) working the penalty box, so she saw everything.

The entire week leading up to our February 19, 2011, bout featuring the Fighting Suzies versus the Monkey Wenches was a rough one. The weekend before, the men's derby team, Rock City Riot, had hosted a recruitment party to which all were invited. To make a long story short — especially short because I don't remember much of it — I drank my weight in vodka, hit my head on the sidewalk — so I'm told — and went to the ER because Miracle, Tool Pelt, and Cheese Degrader said I wouldn't wake up.

School that week had seemed more challenging than usual. I'd had a difficult time listening in class and, in regard to reading and writing, I had the attention span of a goldfish.

Though I hadn't been feeling particularly great, the upcoming bout was one I didn't want to miss. My team, the Fighting Suzies, would already be down in roster numbers because half the team would be saving up energy to play in the A travel team game against Bemidji immediately following the Suzies/Wenches bout. In the home team world, this bout was crucial for the Suzies because the winning team would go on to play in the home team championship, pivotal for bragging rights.

It's the evening of the big bout and while I'm on the track warming up, Nitro Drip (a former skater now ref/paramedic) calls me over from the designated medical spot near the track. *Oooh crap*, I think to myself.

"How's it going, Toni?" she asks as I skid to a stop on one knee.

"Fine," I say, spitting out my mouth guard.

"Heard you had a little accident last weekend."

*Crap, crap, crap . . . how'd she hear about it!? Play it cool, just play it cool.* "Yah, a little whoops I guess."

"Have you been having any headaches?"

*Yes.* "Nope."

"Any troubles concentrating?"

*Uh-huh.* "Nope."

"Sensitivity to light or sounds?"

*Jeeze how'd you know!?* "Nope."

Nitro Drip looks at me and I force out a little smile. *Please let me skate, please let me skate.*

"All right," she says. "Just thought I'd check in with you."

I stand up to skate away but pause. "How'd you hear about last weekend anyway?" I say, turning around toward Nitro. "Who told you?"

She smiles, "Oh, I have my ways, Toni. Let's just say you've got a lot of people concerned about you."

The first half of the bout is exhausting. With only eight skaters on the track, the Suzies struggle to stay alive against the Wenches, who aren't hurting in roster numbers. I've been out on the floor jamming mainly every other jam, and in between jamming I've been blocking. Once in a great while I have a second to sit on the bench, but otherwise the first half of the bout seems like The Déjà 500.

During halftime in the hallway, I try to stretch and keep my head in the game. I feel a bit woozy and light-headed, but shake it off figuring it's probably just a side-effect from all of the jamming. To add more stress to the bout, I overhear the Pains' travel team captains yelling at two Suzies skaters, telling them they're supposed to save their jamming energy for the travel team bout, not this one. This is another negative to not being drafted onto the A team — a constant feeling that any other bout (outside of A team) doesn't matter.

A couple jams in to the second half, it's my turn to jam. I line up on the jammer line, the ref's whistle sounds and I take off down the track. The next thing I remember is a bright flash of light.

[RACHEL'S POINT OF VIEW: "I'm not entirely sure how you managed to fall backwards, but you did, and you hit your head. You tried getting up once, fell, then tried getting up again and fell. You stayed down."]

"Hey Sam, Sammi . . . what month it is?" says a gray-bearded man hovering over me.

For a moment, I think he might be Jesus. But then I notice he's wearing glasses, and I don't recall any pictures of Jesus ever wearing glasses.

"Sammi, what month is it?" he says again.

"Um," *God what month is it?* "Marrr . . . um . . . February," I say. I feel a tug on my arm and look over to see Twizzle, my captain, pulling off my wrist guard.

"Why are you crying?" I ask.

"Because I like you!" she says with a sob.

[RACHEL'S POINT OF VIEW: "Then they put you on a stretcher and took you toward the back exit by the band stage."]

I realize I'm in the back of the Civic Center tied down to a stretcher. I'm freezing cold because it's March or February or whatever fucking cold month it is, and the giant garage door is wide open. A medical guy squeezes my bicep with a blood pressure gauge, and I can feel my cheeks are wet with tears. I look around to notice Rachel standing close by, a grim expression on her face. I look back at the vaulted ceiling and notice Ya'll's Mom standing over me, rubbing my arm.

"Hey you," she says softly in her southern drawl. "Do you want me to call your sister?"

"No. And don't tell anyone I'm crying," I say.

"Okay hun, I won't tell anybody."

I'm wheeled out into the cold night air and put into an ambulance. People talk over the radio in the ambulance, but I can't make out what they're saying.

"Where are you from?" one of the paramedics asks.

"Austin."

"Minnesota?" he asks. "Where they make SPAM?"

"Yup. SPAM capital of the world."

Inside the ER, a lady asks me my name and if I remember anything that happened. I tell her about the white flash of light.

Rachel comes into the room and sits on a chair. "I didn't know you were here," I say.

"I rode in the front of the ambulance," she replies. "How are you feeling?"

"I'm fine. Can we go?" I ask.

"Whenever the doctor says it's okay."

The doctor walks in and informs me he's not going to order a CT scan because, since I had one last weekend, he doesn't want to send me home "glowing." He also mentions that I need to take a two-month break from roller derby.

"TWO MONTHS?! Haha yeah right!" I yell wide-eyed.

The doctor continues yapping, going on and on about how this is my second concussion within a week and something about permanent damage, and too many bonks to the head—all of which seem relatively minor compared to NOT BEING ABLE TO PLAY DERBY FOR TWO MONTHS. "I'm also suggesting that someone wake you up every three hours tonight, or for at least the first twenty-four hours," he says.

"She can stay with me," Rachel says from her seat beside my bed.

"Oh, and by the way," the doctor says before walking out the door, "absolutely no alcohol tonight."

Because both Rachel and I took the ambulance to the hospital, Thunder Thighs (who'd been taking stats during the bout) picks us up in her truck. Walking through the exit of the ER a cold blast of air hits me. I have no jacket, I'm wearing shorts, and somehow I still have my kneepads on.

Thighs offers me a "Gatorade" as I buckle my seatbelt.

"Wait, is that *really* Gatorade?" Rachel asks leaning forward from the back seat.

I take a drink and wrinkle my face. It's Thighs's usual — Gatorade with vodka.

"Give me that!" Rachel yells grabbing the plastic bottle from my hand.

Back at the Civic Center Rachel, Thighs, and I sit on the main stage to catch the final half of the No Pains game against Bemidji. One of the announcers (who I will later find out thought I was dead on the track) notices our presence and informs the crowd that Toni Crush is back and still alive. Everyone cheers.

After the No Pains win, we skip the after party (not my choice), and Rachel and Arizona take me over to their place. During the drive, my head aches and I want nothing more than to go to bed.

I've left the Vicodin from last week's ER visit in my derby bag, so I take some as I'm crawling under the covers of the guest bed. As I'm dozing off Rachel steps into the room and says, "Sam, I'm going to wake you up every three hours, so don't get mad when I do."

"Okay," I mutter.

When I wake up, the ceiling looks different than it did when I'd closed my eyes. I crane my neck and realize there are plastic tubes sticking out of my arms. I notice Rachel sitting across the room, pressing buttons on my Blackberry.

"Who are you texting and why are we ALWAYS here?" I ask, sitting up.

"Hey there," Rachel says looking up from my phone. "You're back in the hospital because you wouldn't wake up. Arizona and I brought you in. Do you remember anything?"

I think for a moment. "I remember falling asleep," I say.

"And then you wouldn't wake up," Rachel says.

"Well did you *try* to wake me up? My mom always said a bomb could go off and I'd sleep right through it."

"Arizona and I tried everything, but you still wouldn't wake up."

This whole wouldn't-wake-up scenario puzzles me. "Wait, what day is it!?" I blurt out. "Oh my God, did I miss classes?"

"It's Sunday," Rachel says typing away on my phone.

"You didn't tell me who you were texting," I say.

"Your mom."

"Wait! What? My MOM? What the fuck?"

"I had to call her because Arizona and I thought you were going to die. So, when I called, your dad answered."

"Oh great," I say. "My parents, especially my mom, didn't need to know about any of this until it was all done and over with," I yell. "She'll lose her mind."

"We had to tell them something, Sam," she says. I know Rachel is serious when she refers to me using my real name as opposed to my derby name.

I lie back in the hospital bed and sigh. "Okay I'm ready to go."

I get discharged from the hospital — my third discharge within an eight-day span — and go back over to Rachel and Arizona's. I haven't eaten since before last night's bout, so we stop at the grocery store for a frozen pizza. I'm not hungry but I eat a slice of pizza before dozing off on the living room couch.

The following day I end up relocating to my home team captain's house. Twizzle's husband is home for the week following a routine surgery, and because I'm still having a hard time waking up and staying awake, and because Rachel and Arizona are both at work all day, it made more sense for me to stay at a location where I'd be in the company of someone else.

For the next few days, I sleep in Twizzle and Rod's guest bedroom and shuffle between movies in front of the downstairs TV to sitcoms and Discovery Channel shows with Rod in front of the upstairs TV. My professors on campus are aware of the situation, thanks to an email sent by Rachel, so I dodge classes all week.

On one evening when Mom calls to check in, she tells me Dad wants to talk to me.

"Really, why?" I say. "He never wants to talk on the phone."

"Oh, he just has something he wants to ask you quick. Here he is," she says, the phone ruffling.

"Hi, kid," Dad says in a cheery voice.

"Hey, Dad, how's it going?"

"Good, good, just got home from work. Say, I just wanted to see if I was gonna have to call Johnny Mayer for ya," he says starting to chuckle.

I smile and let out a snicker. Johnny Mayer was the founder of Mayer Funeral Home in Austin and, as a kid, whenever I was sick with a cold or the flu and home from school, Dad would always joke, "Want me to call Johnny Mayer for ya?" The question used to make me livid when I was little.

"No, no, I don't think you need to this time," I say, "As far as I can tell, my head's still attached."

The sound of Dad's deep laughing — where his voice gets hoarse — fills my earpiece and makes me laugh out loud.

"Okay, kid, just thought I'd ask. Hope you're feeling better. Here's Mom again," he says.

The problem with getting two concussions in a row is that it gets in the way of your usual life. First off, you have to deal with an overabundance of missed phone calls and texts from your mother who is a full time professional worrier of her youngest child. You have to tell her that you're feeling better and you're resting and that no, she doesn't need to drive all the way up to Fargo to make sure you're okay. You tell her it's all right she wasn't able to come to Fargo on the Sunday when Rachel informed her of the incident. You remind her that that's the way the winter weather months are, unpredictable with blizzards that strike when you least expect them. Then you remind your mother that you're in Fargo for grad school, that you didn't move this far away from her for no good reason.

Second, you have to go through all the loopholes to get back into derby practices. You have to tell everyone you're feeling better, which you sort of are but not entirely, while assuring your fellow concerned league mates that yes, you did purchase a new helmet. Then you have to sneak into a Fresh Meat practice here and there so that you can skate a few laps by yourself, no contact with other skaters, and quickly get over that fear of the initial first fall after a serious injury. Then you have to go through all the trouble of getting a clearance note from your doctor that says you're eligible to skate again, that you're no longer at risk for another concussion. Your primary doctor happens to be gone the week after concussion week when you want the approval letter, so you decide on a walk-in-clinic to see a Doc-in-the-Box where he asks you a few questions, makes you balance on one leg with your eyes closed, then clears you for contact. And, of course, you've brought your derby wife along to act as a witness.

The third problem with getting two concussions in a row is that it turns you into a pea-brained, moody, want-to-be recluse who can only come out at night because bright light hurts your eyes. You're in the spring semester of your third year of grad school, and you go from never missing a beat and getting A's to skipping class and getting incompletes on assignments that eventually lead to failed courses. Reading is difficult because you can't concentrate long enough on the page to comprehend what's trying to be said. Paying attention in class is a daunting task, and the notebooks you used to fill with class notes and interesting points of view become notebooks filled with pages of meaningless doodles. Realizing what is happening makes you mad and throws you into an inner war. The mood swings are intense, especially when you go out drinking. You know you shouldn't be drinking, that you should give your brain some rest so it can heal. But you go out drinking anyway. One minute you're a happy drunk who is buying your friends another round, and the next minute you've wandered three blocks from the bar and find yourself crying over the railings of a bridge and looking down into the dark moving current trying to combat the voice inside that is saying, *Jump*.

It will take well over a year for these side effects to wear off. Within that timeframe, you will have filed and been granted retroactive withdrawals from classes; you will have added another dose of antidepressants to your usual morning routine; you will have consumed an ocean of booze and spent a small fortune at the bar; to friends you will have said hurtful words you can't recall during drunken blackout nights; and you will walk away with visible scars on your body that only the keenest of eyes see.

# A Job

Into the spring months, my hours working for Drift Prairie Cleaners trickle down to nothing. Though I hadn't worked much for Diane during the school months, just a part day every Friday, the fact that I was no longer needed irked me. I had always enjoyed the cleaning job, and even though it only paid ten dollars an hour, the satisfaction I got from turning someone's messy house into a shiny and sparkling work of art balanced out the small monetary compensation.

While perusing around for random jobs, I find one that sparks my interest, a temporary part-time job for a local publication just outside of Fargo. I'm flabbergasted that the Fargo-Moorhead area actually produces a magazine besides *Apartment Finder*. I shoot my resume and a short email to the publication to express my interest in the position. A few weeks later I sit in a wood-floored office being interviewed by the editor in chief, let's call him Dwayne.

"We distribute bi-monthly throughout the F-M area," Dwayne says presenting the most current issue on his mahogany desk. He slides the magazine toward me.

"Wow, I like the cover," I pick up the full-size issue and look closer. The cover features a log cabin with a lake off in the distance.

"Basically, *Gone Fishin'* is a magazine that brings together the best elements of the northern great outdoors. We cover every-thing from cabins and pontoons to snowmobiles and cross coun-try skiing," Dwayne says smiling.

I nod my head impressed to learn that there are actually other things to do around the area besides the bars.

Dwayne informs me that while he can't offer me much money — just $250 per month — and the position is very part time — maybe a few hours a day — he'd love for me to join the magazine's team.

Over the next few months, I move up quickly in ranks at the magazine. I go from helping to edit a few articles here and there, to writing articles, to interviewing people for stories, to becom-ing an assistant editor. The other editor, Cody, and I plan feature stories and articles for the magazines, arrange photo shoots, and interview people.

Working for the magazine morphs into a full-time job and pretty soon I find myself in the office working forty-plus hours per week. While the work is fun, the one part that gets under my skin is the fact that my wage has hardly improved. Doing the math one day, Cody and I come to find out that for all of the brainstorming, researching, writing, editing, interviewing, and photo shoot organizing/directing we do, our hourly wage is a measly $7.35 per hour.

Dwayne has a smooth way with words and somehow I always end up taking the bait. Every couple months when I get up the nerve to storm into his office and demand he give me a raise or I quit, he goes into the routine talk of, *the magazine is doing well and people are wanting to advertise through us; the company is in the process of acquiring another popular local magazine and once the deal is sealed we'll have more money to offer to staff; just hang in a little bit longer . . . heck, I didn't even cut myself a paycheck last month so that I could pay everyone else working.* Dwayne saying he "didn't cut himself a paycheck last month" always makes me feel bad, so I inevitably agree to keep writing for the magazine, selling my creative ideas, hard work, and soul for $7.35 an hour.

# Johnny Mayer

It's a sunny spring morning, Good Friday on the Catholic calendar. I'm on campus working on a poetry assignment when I get the call.

"Hey Mom," I say putting the phone on my shoulder while flipping through an anthology of poems that's as heavy as a bowling ball. It's not unusual for Mom to call early in the morning and I figure that since I'm going home over the weekend for Easter she's probably calling to remind me to bring home her pie tin, or her brownie pan, or some other container she'd sent back with me that had been filled with something sweet.

"Hey," she says, her voice rushed.

"What's wrong?"

"It's your father."

A sinking sensation hits my stomach and again I ask what's wrong.

"Well, you know he hasn't been feeling very good lately. He had that cold, which turned into a terrible cough he's had for weeks. So this morning, between appointments, he decided to go down to see his doctor."

Dad isn't one to visit the doctor, especially during workdays when he has clients in and out for haircuts, and *especially* on the Friday before Easter Sunday when he's booked solid. Dad taking time away from work to go to the doctor meant something was very, very wrong.

"They said it was pneumonia and sent him home with some antibiotics. But then, as he was driving home — you know, he thinks he has to go see that doctor all the way down in Adams, oh what's her name? . . . Mary . . . because he's seen her forever . . ."

I interrupt Mom, "Yeah, yeah yeah. So then what?"

"So then as he's driving back home he gets a phone call from Mary at the clinic who tells him she thinks he's got blood clots, of all things, in his lungs and that he needs to head straight for the hospital."

"Blood clots? In his lungs? I didn't know that was a thing," I say.

"Well, it is. So he's checked himself into the hospital, and I'm on my way down there right now," she says.

"Okay. So what are they going to do?"

"I'm not quite sure, but I'll find out more when I get there. Listen sweetie, I've got to go. I already talked to Jen, but I'm going to call your brother now to let him know the situation."

"Well, do you think I should come home right now?" I ask. I hadn't planned on leaving town until Saturday because I had some schoolwork to finish.

"No, no, not right now. Just keep your plans of coming down tomorrow."

"Are you sure?" I say in a hesitant tone.

"Yes, yes. I've got to go. I'll call you later."

I hang up with Mom and Google "blood clots in lungs." There's a wealth of information on the subject. The Mayo Clinic website refers to the condition as Pulmonary Embolism, a term I vaguely remember from health classes during my undergrad.

For as long as I can remember, Dad has smoked either his tobacco pipe or Swisher Sweets Cigars. When I was little, I remember sitting inside the porch with Dad while he smoked his pipe. Mom didn't allow smoking inside the house, so Dad was limited to outside or the three seasons porch attached to our house.

When I think back to Dad's pipe-smoking days, it's always a warm summer evening and I'm sitting across the porch table from him. He's in his bathrobe and I'm in my pajamas. The porch windows are open and the sounds of crickets surround us. In my hand I hold a small plastic pipe, a bubble pipe that holds soap water in one end and releases bubbles into the air when I blow through it from the other end. As Dad takes a puff from his pipe, I take a puff from my bubble pipe, which is soap free because bubbles aren't allowed in the porch. He exhales and I exhale. The air is filled with a sweet aroma of tobacco and cherry. We sit in silence, Dad looking out the windows into the backyard, me watching the embers in his pipe and the endless trail of smoke wafting toward the ceiling.

Later, after Dad's pipe-smoking days came his Swisher Sweets days. At first, he only smoked them whenever gambling was involved: the horse track, the dog track, and Mystic Lake Casino. Then, slowly the cigars started making a few more appearances: in the boat while fishing, during hiking trips, while camping in the woods. Once, when my cousin and I were frog hunting on the weedy shores of a lake, Dad was following behind us, smoking a cigar. Suddenly there was a loud thump followed by the whooshing of weeds, crackling of twigs, and another large thump. When I turned around to see what the commotion was, Dad had completely vanished. Frozen in fear that a bear had attacked Dad, the weeds began to shake and the twigs began to snap and suddenly he rose from the weeds, a smashed cigar hanging between his lips. Of course, when Mom later heard this story she was more than thrilled to use this as further evidence to support her redundant message of "Those damn cigars will kill you."

But, still un-phased by Mom's harassment, Dad continued smoking the Swisher Sweets until they were finally around for every occasion. Evidence of how many cigars he smoked over the winter months reared its ugly head every spring when the snow melted away to reveal white plastic cigar tips scattered throughout the backyard. And while he picked them up as best he could, trying to get rid of the evidence, every so often when Dad would be mowing the summer lawn, a sudden *click, clack, clack* would resonate from the innards of the lawn mower and be followed by a *ka-ching* as a plastic tip would shoot across the yard.

The rest of the morning I'm unable to focus on my homework. I have more questions so I call Mom a couple times, but she doesn't answer. I send her a text and get no reply. It's pointless trying to get any sort of work done today, so I pack up my books and head back to my apartment.

During my drive, as I ponder the idea of whether I should head down to Austin this afternoon, a faint aroma of cigar smoke suddenly wafts through my car as I stop at a red light. The smoke smells exactly like Dad. The scent disappears as quickly as it arrived, and I instantly burst into tears because I think I may have just lost my father.

Mom calls me back as I pull into a parking spot at my apartment. She tells me that Dad was taken over to Mayo in Rochester via ambulance and was now on blood thinners in the hospital.

"Hey Dad," I say through my phone. It's early Friday evening and Dad's finally feeling well enough to talk.

"Hey kid," he says, his voice is unfamiliar — soft and weak.

Because I'm terrible with serious and emotional situations, I say the only thing that comes to mind, "So do I need to call Johnny Mayer for ya?" I've inherited my father's knack for smoothing over an emotional situation with a bad joke, a realization that makes me cry even harder.

Dad chuckles lightly over the phone and I picture him rolling his eyes.

He tells me he's feeling better, that he's on a heavy dose of blood thinners, and that he should be out of the hospital in a day or two.

"I really thought I was going to be sleeping alone that night," Mom says to me from across the porch table, a cup of coffee in her hands.

It's Easter Sunday, and I've just gotten home from mass with my brother and his family. My nieces are chaotic as usual, running around in the backyard playing in their Easter dresses and blowing bubbles the Easter Bunny had left.

Dad sits in a chair beside me. His face is pale and he looks more drained and tired than I can ever remember, though he insists he's feeling a lot better.

"It was weird not having the two of you at church this morning," I say to change the subject.

Dad says, "This is probably the first time we've ever missed Easter Mass, isn't that right Berta?" He looks at Mom.

"Yeah, I think so," she replies, sipping her coffee.

# Four Loko

"I wanna try that Four Loko stuff everybody's always talking about," Swear Jar says unstrapping her knee pad. Travel team practice has just let out and a bunch of us are de-gearing.

"Didn't they ban that stuff in some states?" Margo-Forehead asks.

"You bet your ass they did. But you know one place where they didn't ban it?" Swear Jar widens her eyes and grins, "North Dakota. I hear you can get shit-faced drunk off just one can," she holds up her pointer finger and raises her eyebrows.

Swear Jar has one of the most animated faces I've seen. If she was ever to permanently lose her voice she'd have no trouble communicating her thoughts via her eyes and eyebrows.

"We should plan a Four Loko night," she says, "what's everybody doing this Friday?"

It's a warm Friday evening and the street lamps are just starting to turn on. Swear Jar arrives at our agreed-upon pre-game spot — a parking lot outside of a downtown bar — with not one, not two, but three cans of Four Loko, all different flavors. Instead of drinking just one at a time, she cracks open all three and passes them around our group.

I take a sip of the watermelon flavored Four Loko and scrunch my nose. "Ish, I dunno about that stuff, Swear Jar," I say, sticking out my tongue.

"Eh, try the berry flavored. I think it tastes better. Margo, give Toni a sip of the berry-flavored one."

"Here Toni, try this," Margo-Forehead smiles and hands me the can.

I take a swig. "Yeah, that doesn't taste much better either," I say and stick out my tongue.

"Yeah, I've definitely tasted better," Swear Jar says waving her can around, "but to think you can get shit-faced drunk for less than five dollars? That's amazing! God, I love North Dakota."

Later that evening, Margo turns out to be the one who gets completely hammered. Sitting with her back against a wall in an alley, she is practically toppling over. None of us have ever seen Margo this drunk and when her husband arrives to bring her home, we cheer to her drunkenness as she trips into the passenger seat of their car.

Swear Jar sneaks cans of Four Loko into every bar we hit that night. I continue to drink the stuff, though it tastes bad, but I'm drunk, so who cares. As the night wears on, the drunken asshole in me awakens from hell — a horrible side effect of too much hard alcohol — and before I know it I'm pissing people off.

I tell one of the new girls on the league that she's kind of cocky, because she is. She's a good skater and she's young, but she's a little too proud for my taste. I try nicely to say, "You're cocky," but trying to nicely tell someone they're cocky isn't easy. In fact, it's rather blunt. And even more blunt when you're drunk. But, when you're drunk, you don't realize how blunt it is. After I tell her the news she looks at me and nods. A good sign, I assume. Not really. Later that night we head over to a Merby-guy's house, and I later hear through the grapevine that "Cocky" is crying and is upset. But I don't care, I think she deserves it. I crawl up onto the roof of the rambler we're partying at and pass out for a while.

# Nineteen Ways to Be a Drunk Asshole:

1. Pass out in a snow bank.
2. Drive your car into another car, exit car, retrieve your car's front bumper from road, place in back seat, flee scene, phone friend from jail at 4:00 a.m. asking for $500 bail bond.
3. Share can of Four Loko with derby friends.
4. Inform someone nobody likes her because she comes off as "cocky."
5. Share second can of Four Loco with friends.
6. Pass out on the roof of a house.
7. Tell one drunk you're too drunk to drive so he should, get in car with said drunk who decides to crash into parked car, quickly dispose of alcohol evidence in nearest random trash can, fifteen seconds later retrieve said evidence from nearest random trash can, carry and dump evidence in blue bin labeled *Aluminum Recycling*.
8. Get so loosey goosey from combination of two little blue pills and ten very large mugs that you slide backward off bar stool.
9. Pass out in a random bush.
10. Pee behind a dumpster in a dark downtown alley.
11. When knock on door is followed by deep bellowing voice yelling, "Campus Security," flee to nearest closet for safety.
12. Punch guy in face for reason you can't recall.
13. After seven hours of partying at bar, buy case of Miller Lite at

1:59 a.m. for the after party.

14. Show up to writing workshop drunk out of mind because you can't bear to listen to professor's voice.

15. Send 3 a.m. email to rep at temp work agency and regret you cannot make 8 a.m. work tomorrow, which is really today in five hours, because you have booze — I mean food — poisoning.

16. Forget about cheese sandwich placed in microwave, make second cheese sandwich because you can't figure out where first cheese sandwich went, forget about second cheese sandwich and pass out in bed. Wake up next afternoon to discover mysterious cheese sandwich in microwave.

17. Make best friend cry for reasons you can't remember. Wake up next day and ask why best friend is *acting so distant*.

18. Push someone into a fence then make out with her.

19. Attempt to ride home in sober driver's trunk.

# Rachel Moving

Rachel's decision to move out west to attend graduate school in Washington doesn't come as a complete shock, but it hurts me nonetheless. She'd been a straight-A student during her undergrad and already had a couple years of experience working in a career field that encouraged a graduate education. Rachel applies to a few different programs around the country and is offered scholarships to each. One school is on the east coast, the other on the west coast, and the other just across town.

Everything in me wants her to stay. To go to my school, to continue skating at FMDG, to stay in her townhouse with Arizona so that I can continue to hang out with Henry on weekdays. I try to remain neutral on the subject of her leaving. I tell her that if she stays in town and goes to school across the river everything can stay the same. I also tell her that if she's up for a change of scenery, I'll support her with that decision too.

Rachel had lived in Washington for a few years before I met her. She told me she always liked it out there, that the mountains were pretty and the winters weren't as cold and long as they were in Fargo. I'd been to Seattle to visit my cousins a few times, and while I did like the scenery, I knew the weather was cloudy and dismal during the winter months. Not that it wasn't cloudy and dismal in Fargo during winter, but there was usually a fresh blanket of snow on the ground to brighten things up a bit, as opposed to the never-ending Seattle drizzle.

Arizona had also caught the graduate school bug and ends up getting accepted to the same Washington school as Rachel. Arizona is a native of southern California and the only reason she'd moved to Fargo was for work straight out of her undergrad. Throughout the winter months, Arizona had bitched and moaned nonstop about the weather — about how stinking cold Fargo was and that people were crazy to live here. It is no surprise to me when she joins Rachel for a long weekend getaway to visit a campus in Washington.

The week after Rachel's return from Washington, I try to avoid the subject of her going to graduate school. Maybe if I don't mention it she'll forget about the whole thing. But she doesn't forget and at the end of summer she and Arizona will move.

My derby wife's decision to move halfway across the country turns me into an emotional wreck. Rachel was someone I felt comfortable opening up to. Though I've always been a person who wears a happy face on the outside, more than half the time I'm actually a complete wreck on the inside. And Rachel was someone in my life with whom I was able to share these feelings with.

The last person I opened up to had been a friend in high school who I had considered to be a best friend. But as I grew older and expanded my circle of friends and my understanding of friendship respect, I came to realize our relationship was one-sided and that my other friends didn't treat me the way she always did. Her verbal, and at one point, physical abuse was not something my college friends did to me. They didn't make me feel bad about the clothes I wore or the books I read. They didn't take their anger and frustrations out on me by calling me "dyke" and "idiot." After deciding to call it off with this high school friend and to drop all lines of communication with her, a part of me felt like I had been taken away, like all of me that I had shared with her was now hers, and I could never have it back. I had made myself vulnerable by giving away too much of myself. And that hurt.

With Rachel planning to move in August, I feel like she, too, will take a part of me when she leaves. We had built a genuine friendship that, at times, seemed to tip beyond friendship. The fact that she was willing to walk away so easily felt like a skate to the gut.

# A Bad Night

I sit on the edge of the bathtub holding the razor to my left wrist. My head spins and hot tears stream down my cheeks. Drunk. Sad. Angry. I want these feelings out of my body.

I hadn't felt like myself all week. A mixture of having, yet again, missed the cut for the A team, and learning that Rachel was accepting her full ride to a graduate school—located 1,300 miles away in the foothills of some mountain range with a name I couldn't pronounce—caught up to me. I'd gone out drinking nearly every night of the week, not necessarily getting shit-faced drunk, because I usually saved that for a Friday or Saturday night, but drunk enough to be drunk. Thinking that being around people might help take the edge off my emotions, I had decided to head downtown for drinks with Miracle and some of the Merby guys.

Early in the evening, I'd met Miracle at her apartment and we'd gone over to a cash-only hole-in-the-wall bar known for its extra strong pours. Instead of ordering my usual beer, I chose to start out with a Long Island Iced Tea, which, after tasting, was pure alcohol with a touch of ice.

As the night wore on, with every sip of alcohol I felt myself drifting further from my surroundings. Faces became fuzzy, words sounded foreign, music from the live band sounded like one continuous note. By bar close, I was hammered but decided to head over to Miracle's with her and a couple other Merby guys for more drinking.

The first slice makes me wince in pain, but I pull my elbow tight to my side, steady my wrist, and swipe again. Red oozes up out of the parted layers of skin, and I close my eyes because I can't stand the sight of the blood. I don't cut to watch myself bleed; I cut to *feel* myself bleed. Steadying myself on the side of Miracle's bathtub, I ease into its empty basin and slump down, resting my shoulders against its smooth edges. I have to rest for a second, to sit back and get my heavy breathing under control. After a moment, I decide I need one more swipe to make sure everything gets out. Another slice deepens the cut, the red flowing more easily this time, trickling down my arm. I close my eyes.

A loud banging jolts me awake and I open my eyes to Miracle kneeling beside the bathtub.

"Sammi, what's going on?"

"I'm fine," I say, my eyes burning from tears forming.

Miracle is quiet and reaches across my body to grab my hand. My wrist is red and drips with blood.

The bathroom door makes a soft creak, and I see Paul, a Merby skater, stick his head in.

"Close the fucking door!" I sob.

Paul rushes inside and closes the door behind him. *Fuck, I must have passed out. Fuck fuck fuck.*

"Sammi, you're not fine. What's going on, hun?" Miracle asks, still holding my hand.

I tilt my head toward her hand, "You have blood on you." She doesn't say anything. Paul inches over toward the bathtub and sits down on the floor. His eyes are red with tears.

Silence.

"I don't know what's wrong," I say, "I haven't felt good again. Sometimes everything just gets so sad and shitty, and I don't know why. I can't turn my mind off. I take my meds like I'm supposed to, but sometimes they don't seem to do anything. I'm sorry. You're not supposed to see this. Or deal with this."

Miracle wraps her arms around my upper body and pulls me close to her. My eyes burn and though I try to fight back tears, they keep flowing.

Rubbing a hand across my back, she says, "Let's get you cleaned up and into bed."

Paul grabs one side of me and Miracle grabs the other as I step out of the tub and walk over to the sink. The cold water stings my wrist, but the bleeding has slowed.

"I don't have any Band-Aids," Miracle says, rummaging through her bathroom cabinet. "This should work though." She comes over to me and unwraps a pink Carefree pad. She places the pad over my cuts and wraps it around my wrist. "Hold this," she says. I hold the pad in place and she unwinds a roll of athletic tape, tears off a long piece, and wraps it around the pad on my wrist.

# Those Parades

The following text conversation occurs during an evening when I'm drunk on a mixture of beer, vodka, and country music.

[Mom, Sat. 9:02 p.m.] Hi! Haven't heard from you lately. What have you been up to?

[Me, Sat. 9:04 p.m.] Out at WeFest right now for derby. We got free tix since they're one of our sponsors.

[Mom, Sat. 9:12 p.m.] Sounds like fun. Who are you with?

[Me, Sat. 9:13 p.m.] A Bunch of derby friends. The stage is outside and we're in the middle of a huge crowd of people.

[Mom, Sat. 9:20 p.m.] Okay, well have fun and be safe. ☺

*Six drinks later . . .*

[Me, Sun. 12:01 a.m.] Mom I hav 2 tell u smthing Ive been wanting 2 say 4 a while. Im nevr going to bring anothr guy home.

*Five seconds and no response . . .*

[Me, Sun. 12:01 a.m.] I like women. Im gay.

*Two seconds and still no response . . .*
[Me, Sun. 12:01 a.m.] U don't have anything to say? Jen knows. I tld her a long time ago. If ur not ok with it then im sorry. It's who I am.

[Mom, Sun. 12:02 a.m.] I'm trying to write back but I can't type fast enough to keep up with you.

[Me, Sun. 12:02 a.m.] Oh.

[Mom, Sun. 12:08 a.m.] Sammi that's ok. You know your father and I will support you in whatever you choose and we will love you no matter what.

[Me (crying), Sun. 12:09 a.m.] So ur not mad? Ive been wanting to tell u 4 a while but dnt know how.

[Mom, Sun. 12:13 a.m.] Sweetie, of course I'm not mad.

*A few weeks later . . .*

I sit outside in my parents' backyard, breathing in the warm evening air and admiring the vast array of plants and flowers. The yard looks like something out of a *Better Homes and Gardens* magazine. The porch door opens and Dad walks into the yard.

"Hey kid," he says walking toward me and plopping down in a plastic chair beside mine. "Nice you could come down for a long weekend."

"Yeah, I needed to get out of Fargo for a while."

A few minutes of silence pass between us. As I watch a squirrel run across the top of the wooden fence Dad says, "So, Mom tells me you're gay."

*Ka-bonk!* I feel like I've just been clonked on the head with one of those giant cartoon hammers. So caught off-guard, I sit completely still in my chair, questioning whether or not Dad said what I think he just said.

"Ah . . . yeah . . ." I reply, looking at him.

Dad turns his gaze toward the yard, pauses for a moment, then looks back at me. "I don't care what you do, kid. Do whatever makes you happy," he says.

I nod my head in agreement and smile.

Dad smiles back and says with a chuckle, "But don't think this means I'm going to walk in any of those parades."

# Classless Felon

"So we have a bit of a problem," Ty Kwon Don't says when I answer my phone. It's a sunny fall afternoon and I've just climbed into my car to go grab lunch. Judging by her voice, I sense this might be a long conversation with Ty, who is head of the marketing committee, so I roll down my window and get comfortable. "We think Nina has been stealing money from FMDG," she says.

"What?" I ask. Nina, also known as Mysterious Mist, is the treasurer on the board of directors for FMDG. She had been an active skater in the league for a while, but as of recently had taken to the sidelines due to injuries. "What makes you think she's stealing our money?"

Ty sighs, "The board held an emergency meeting the other night after practice, and while going over some paperwork, Char noticed that things in our bank account weren't adding up. So Gun Hoe went and got statements from the bank and there are all kinds of withdrawals from our account that we never did."

"Withdrawals?" I ask.

"Yes, withdrawals from our account at various ATMs. FMDG had a debit card, and Mist is the only one who has it."

"Well, why in the Christ do we have a debit card? Is that even necessary?" I ask.

Ty sighs again, "I have no idea why, but that's something to ask the board."

For a moment, I mull over things in my mind. "Well, how much do they think she's taken?" I ask.

"It's not for sure yet, but at least a couple thousand dollars."

"A couple THOUSAND dollars? Jesus," I say. "Are you sure it's Mist? I mean, why would she want to steal our money? She's always the one pushing us and reminding us to pay our dues. She's a dues Nazi."

"Nobody else has access to the debit card. And none of the other board members deal with the money. Anyway, I thought I'd call and give you a heads up since you're in training to take over Char's spot as league secretary."

True, I was in training to become FMDG's new league secretary. Char and her girlfriend were planning to move to Wyoming at the end of the year once she finished her PhD program at North Dakota State University. Ever since I'd joined the league, Char had been after me to take her position as secretary. She had dubbed me her "sex-retary" and had recently turned over to me a hefty amount of league paperwork that could undoubtedly fuel a bonfire for a month. Initially, I was hesitant to say I'd take over the position because it seemed like an awful lot of work. But over and over Char had reassured me that I was more than qualified for the position, and upon her showing me some of the ropes of the job, I'd agreed to take over her spot come November. Now I was having second thoughts.

Mist seemed like a good person, someone you wouldn't ever think would do anything behind your back. She had a couple of kids, lived in a nice house, and had recently gotten married. She looked like the type of person who would be an accountant — well-polished business attire, high heels, glasses, a stereotypical accountant look. But then again, maybe some things weren't adding up.

Every few weeks at league meetings, which were open to

all league skaters, the board briefly highlighted the status of FMDG's bank account. With home team season being on pause throughout the spring and summer months, it was expected our bank account did more paying out (mostly toward warehouse rent) than bringing in. During our spring league meetings and early summer meetings whenever Char or Gun Hoe, our league president, would mention our current bank account balance, nobody thought too much about the fact that our funds were steadily dwindling.

By around mid-summer, however, FMDG's finances started becoming a hot topic to talk about amongst league skaters. Where was all our money going? Was it really all going toward rent? Whatever happened to the $5,000 we made selling frozen pizzas in January? Or what about all the money we brought in from selling t-shirts and other merchandise during the season? And remember all those FMDG Christmas ornaments we sold last November? Where had all that profit gone?

For a short while, Mist had made more appearances at the warehouse during travel team practices and open skate times to collect monthly dues. She insisted that if dues were paid in a timely manner it would help our bank account tremendously. Everyone seemed to think she knew what she was doing. After all, she had been the head bookkeeper for a former restaurant in town (before it filed for bankruptcy) AND she knew how to use QuickBooks.

While Mist's resilience to collect money from skaters had increased for a short time, her attendance at board and league meetings had decreased to the point of nonexistence. After months of unanswered phone calls and emails and dodged requests by the board for full detailed budget reports, President Gun Hoe put her foot down and went to the bank to get all of the league's statements. It took three board members to comb through the eighteen-plus months of bank statements to finally reveal that FMDG's treasurer was stealing the league's money.

A week or so after talking with Ty, the Board called an emergency league meeting at the warehouse. Since the email announcing the meeting contained the word *emergency* in the subject line, a huge percentage of league members showed up. It usually took some sort of drastic event to get skaters who weren't on the board to actually attend a league meeting. Sitting toward the back of the room, I'm surrounded by the usual chatter and laughing of fellow league mates. Everyone seemed to be in good spirits except for the four board members and a few other committee heads who were up to date on the news.

"All right everyone," Gun Hoe says, looking around the room. The chatter winds down and people turn toward the front of the room. "Let's get underway with this meeting." Gun Hoe pauses for a brief moment, shakes her head, and lets out a sigh. "I don't really know how to start this so I'm just going to lay it out . . . Mist has been stealing money from the league."

Any remaining chatter amongst meeting attendees stops dead — like in the movies after the invisible record screeches. An eerie silence fills the room and everyone remains frozen in their spots.

"We have credible evidence from our bank account records that show purchases and ATM withdrawals that were never approved by the board," Gun Hoe says fanning through a thick stack of papers. "As of right now, the board has suspended Mist from the league. The evening we found out she'd been stealing our money, we went over to her house and took back her set of warehouse keys, FMDG files, and other FMDG property. The following day we took all of our unauthorized bank charges to the Fargo Police Department and as of now we've hired a detective."

After the meeting I stop at a bar across the street to grab a beer with a few league mates. I pull up a chair next to Char, and she shows me the thick stack of bank papers entailing the withdrawals from FMDG's account.

"How much do you think she's taken?" I ask.

Char shakes her head, "A lot. Thousands and thousands probably. We think she's taken enough money that FMDG might be able to file a lawsuit against her. Anything over $10,000 is considered a felony," she says.

"$10,000!" I practically spit my beer across the table. "You really think she took that much? How come nobody realized she was taking any of our money? Looking at the dates on those pages, she's been doing this for quite a while. Why didn't the board catch on?"

"We had no reason to really be suspicious of anything," Char says and shrugs her shoulders. "It wasn't until this summer when we began questioning Mist about the money in our account that we started to get suspicious. She wouldn't show up for board meetings and every time we'd finally get hold of her to say the board needed copies of the bookwork from her, she'd disappear."

The feud between the Fargo Moorhead Derby Girls and Nina Adler turns out to be a long, drawn-out legal battle. Conclusions resulting from the detective's work and auditing of FMDG's bank records reveal roughly $13,000 in unauthorized transactions. With this amount being well over the felony theft level, FMDG decides to file charges against Nina.

What really fuels FMDG's decision to file charges lies in the fact that the league is a nonprofit organization that provides donations to charities around the Fargo-Moorhead area. At each bout during our regular season play, a local charity is sponsored and a certain percentage of the income earned during that bout goes toward that sponsored charity. FMDG's featured charities have ranged from Firstlink Giving Tree to the Cass-Clay Backpack Program to the Rape and Abuse Crisis Center and many others. FMDG also relies heavily on contracted league sponsors such as local businesses and organizations. These league sponsors provide the league with funds that allow bouts to be put on. To sum it up: with sponsors we bout and with bouts we give money. But now thanks to Nina the formula is all fucked up. Who wants to sponsor a league (or business) that is plagued by newspaper headlines reading "Former treasurer of Fargo-Moorhead roller derby team accused of stealing thousands of dollars." And how is our league supposed to provide money for our upcoming fall charities if we can't afford to put on a bout? And how can we put on a bout if we can't afford to pay rent for our practice space? So in reality, Nina's decision to steal from FMDG had not only affected the league and skaters, but also the community.

Throughout the legal battle, there were a few brief sightings of Nina, who FMDG eventually came to refer to as "Classless Felon." One skater mentioned that she saw Classless Felon at the checkout aisle in the grocery store. Enraged at the sight of the thief—who was possibly buying groceries with FMDG's pocketed money—this skater made a beeline directly toward the thief, and the thief, upon seeing someone quickly approaching her, turned to notice the angry skater and immediately fled the scene leaving her half-bagged groceries behind.

Another skater who was on a weekend excursion to the Twin Cities with her husband claimed to have seen Classless Felon walking along a busy street in downtown Minneapolis. Classless Felon must have concluded that Fargo was too dangerous of a city to live in when angry derby skaters were on the prowl.

Then there were the days FMDG skaters were sure Nina would make an appearance for a scheduled court date. FMDG's Yahoo Group would explode with eager messages asking "What time?" "What day?" and "Should we all meet for lunch before or after court?" And then, the day of court, only Classless Felon's lawyer would show, and league skaters who'd taken time off work to catch a glimpse of the league crook would be stuck sulking into their luncheon beers.

But eventually, the day would finally come when the Fargo Moorhead Derby Girls would win their battle in court. Initially a plea agreement that Nina serve ten days on house arrest and pay back $10,000 was made. But the judge must not have thought that ten days of sitting at home watching soap operas on TV would really help Nina learn the severity of her crime. He sentenced her to twenty days in jail, ten days on house arrest, $10,000 in restitution, and ruled that the felony theft conviction stay on her record. And after all of that, Classless Felon disappeared into a Mysterious Mist.

# Stick it Where the Sun Don't Shine

I hit the silence button on my phone for the fifth time. It's just before lunchtime on a Wednesday, and I'm outside with my dog, Dickens, waiting for him to go potty. My parents would be horrified if they knew what I was doing. They would call it "unacceptable" and "completely unprofessional." And I would agree with them. I would agree that I was being irresponsible, negligent, and careless because at the moment I was skipping work, completely unannounced.

All of the anger and frustration regarding the money (or lack of it) I made at my job as assistant editor for the magazine had finally erupted this morning. Maybe it was the fact that last week Dwayne had decided to hire a couple more employees. If he had the money to hire, why didn't he actually pay the people who already worked for him? Or, maybe I was mad about the four brand new Apple computers (the ones with the extra large screens) that arrived at the office on Monday and were distributed to Dwayne, the graphic designer, and the two sales workers. Where were mine and Cody's new computers? Why were we still doing all the magazine work on personal laptops? Or, maybe I was mad because I was sick of my car's fuel tank always being on E from driving around the area to conduct interviews and distribute magazines. Ironically, my car's gas gauge has been broken since I got the car. The little pointer finger is permanently stuck above the F (full) line. So, while it looks like I have gas, the gauge is really just kidding.

Whatever the exact cause of my anger is, I'm fed up with working for Dwayne. I'm sick of his carrot-dangling tactics and always being led along for just a little bit longer. He had promised and promised but had never actually come through with anything.

After another hour or so of ignoring phone calls, I decide to call someone at the office to inform them that I'm quitting.

"Sammi, where have you been?" Jim, one of the sales guys, asks over the phone. I figured Cody was probably busy doing interviews and that Dwayne was probably in a meeting, so I had decided to call Jim to tell him my ordeal.

I tell him I'm done working for the magazine because I'm sick of not making any money. Jim listens intently, and, when I'm done ranting, there's a brief silence.

"I understand your frustrations, Sammi," Jim says after a moment. "But either way, not showing up to work isn't really the right way to go about this. I'll tell Dwayne you'll give him a call this afternoon to talk things over."

Deep down I know Jim is right. Skipping work is tacky and irresponsible. But in all actuality, I didn't know how else to go about it, how to actually get Dwayne's attention.

Later that afternoon when I call Dwayne, I'm surprised when he answers. Over my ten months of working for the magazine, he'd never once actually picked up the phone when I had called.

"Well, Sammi," he says after listening to me explain the ordeal, "I really wish you would have come to me sooner about this. Maybe we could have worked something out."

At this instant if I could have punched him over the phone I would have. Had he completely forgotten about the numerous times I had gone in to his office to talk about a raise? Who the fuck had I been conversing with during those times? A cardboard cutout?

Instead of reminding Dwayne about the countless times I'd asked for a raise, I thank him for the opportunity and wish him the worst —I mean best — of luck with the magazine.

# Missed Again

According to an email I receive on my phone, for the third time in a row I have not make the A team.

I've been downtown all evening catching up with Char and her girlfriend who were back in town from Wyoming to celebrate Char's graduation from her PhD program. Over the course of the night, between discussions of politics, economics and, of course, roller derby, I had repeatedly checked my phone for an email, the email that would announce season four's A-team and B-team rosters. The training committee and the former A- and B-team captains and co-captains had been in a meeting since early evening discussing and deciding where skaters who had tried out for travel teams belonged. Tryouts had gone exceptionally well, in my opinion, and I had skated great both nights, even setting a new personal record of thirty-four laps in five minutes, something only one A-team skater had achieved. My hits had been solid thanks to hours spent at the gym lifting weights, and I'd gotten lead jammer a handful of times each night. I was certain I had finally secured a spot on the Northern Pains roster. After all, the roster could hold up to twenty skaters and a fair number of them had quit or transferred or moved.

When a few of the skaters who had been at the meeting arrived at the bar, I knew the email was sure to follow. Sure enough, the little red light on my phone began to blink and I fumbled with it trying to hit the open button as fast as possible. It read something along the lines of "Introducing this season's travel team roster." I had scanned down the lines reading off the names of A-team skaters who'd again, made the A team. My name wasn't on it. I continued scrolling down to find my name under the column titled "Furies."

I scroll through the email again, counting skaters and making sure I haven't missed anything. No matter how many times I re-read the email, my name remains in the column that says "Furies Roster."

"Ah, what changed?" I say out loud to a skater who has just come from the meeting. She looks at me as I continued, "There's only one new person on the A team?" I say. "Why are there *only* fourteen skaters when the roster can hold up to twenty?"

"You'll have to wait for your evaluation," she says and sips her drink. "They're being sent to all skaters who tried out for both travel teams."

I look at her for a moment, dumbfounded, then decide it's time to go. I have to get out of the bar.

I pretend I'm going to use the restroom and burst out the door into the night air. I pull my sweatshirt hood over my head and begin walking wherever my feet will take me. I stop behind a parking lot dumpster. I don't know what to do, the anger and frustration inside feels unbearable. I want to explode. I take out my phone and soon I'm sitting on the rocky parking lot ground, leaning up against a green rusted dumpster and crying over the line to my derby wife.

"I don't understand *why the fuck* I can't make the stupid A team," I sob and wipe my nose on my shirt neck.

"I can't believe they only took fourteen skaters," Rachel says. "Why would they do that? It doesn't make much sense to me."

"I don't know why either," I mumble. "And I don't know why they wouldn't take a skater who got thirty-four laps in five minutes."

"You got thirty-four in five?" she asks, a touch of awe in her voice.

"Yeah," I say, crying harder. "And they said they were going to take into account endurance and attendance and attitude and all the stuff I'm told I'm good at. And I still don't make it."

After a pause, Rachel says, "That's total bullshit."

I'm tired and my eyes are about to pop out of my head from crying. I tell Rachel I'm taking a cab home and going to bed.

"You know," she says before we hang up, "you should really come skate out here in Washington."

# TURN FOUR: CALLING OFF THE JAM

# The Move

One afternoon I call up Rachel and tell her I'm ready to take her offer and move to Washington. That spring had been my final semester of coursework for the graduate program I was enrolled in. All that was left for my master's was to complete the thesis, a task that could be done anywhere. I had quit my assistant editor job a couple months ago, so no job was keeping me tied to Fargo. But most of all, I was done with FMDG. I felt stuck in a rut with my skating, frustrated that nobody took me seriously. I'd burned a lot of bridges with my drinking, and I knew it. But I'd also put in a lot of dedication to the league and my skating.

Rachel listens intently over the phone, "Well, if you think this is what you want to do, then by all means come on out. But remember what I told you over the summer," her tone is serious. What Rachel is about to say is something I hoped she had forgotten. It was something I didn't want to hear and something I was afraid to stand up to. "If you're going to move out here," she continues, "you can't drink the way you do in Fargo."

Over the four years I've spent living in my tiny south Far-ghetto apartment, I've accumulated a lot of shit. Everywhere I turn there are books. They're under the TV, under the bed, on the dusty kitchen table I never use, in the corner behind my bike, and at the bottom of my closet beneath clothes I haven't worn for two years.

The moving process turns into a sort of cleansing process. I fill trash bags with clothes and shoes I haven't worn in years and drop them off in donation bins. I hook friends up with furniture I no longer need. I stack small piles of books beside the dumpster outside my apartment knowing that people will come along and take what they're interested in. Lonny Blossoms helps me carry out the final touch to the dumpster library — a brown leather chair, otherwise known as my TV chair. The dumpster area looks exactly like my apartment, only outside.

"I'm sure gonna miss you Sammi Jones," Lonny says as he plops the bulky chair next to a stack of books. It's a muggy September evening in 2012, and Lonny and I are sweating from having carried the chair out.

"I think I'm ready to get out of Fargo," I say, wiping a drop of sweat with my shirtsleeve.

Lonny has helped pack my car and it's so full I half expect the tires to pop. Over the previous weeks I'd made numerous trips down to the Twin Cities to my sister's house to store things in her garage that I'd eventually take down to Mom and Dad's in Austin. Lonny tugs at the strings on my bike rack making sure everything is secure. The previous weekend my family had given me a bike rack for my twenty-eighth birthday, and tonight I was putting it to good use.

"Well, I think that's about it," I say looking at my car.

"Don't forget that little man over there," Lonny points toward a tree. While packing the car, I had leashed Dickens to a tree because whenever Lonny and I would leave the apartment Dickens would have a bark attack.

"How could I ever forget a face as cute as that," I say undoing the leash.

"Well kid, I've got to get going. Mary and the kids are going to be home soon," Lonny says, extending his arms out for a hug.

"Yeah, we better be hitting the road," I say giving him a bear

hug. "I think D and I will do one last sweep of the apartment before we head down to my sister's."

"What day did you say you're driving out to Washington?"

"Monday my mom and I are going to leave. She's going to
drive out there with me to keep D and me company. One of her
sisters lives in Seattle, so we'll stay there for a few days and then
I'll drop her off at the airport on my way to Rachel's."

"That'll be a nice little trip for the two of you."

"I think so too. She's all nervous about me leaving, so I guess
it makes sense for her to come out to see where I'm going to
be living."

Dickens and I make one last run-through of our efficiency apartment. Minus a few spots on the carpet, the place looks like it
did when I moved in on a humid August day in 2008. Looking
around a sudden heaviness hits my stomach. Am I ready to say
goodbye to Fargo? Am I ready to start a new chapter? Am I ready
to move halfway across the country?

# The Dog House

My first week in Washington is off to a rough start. Upon my arrival, Rachel informs me that it makes more sense for me to sleep in Arizona's room since her room is bigger. Earlier in the year when I had flown out to visit, Rachel had said that if I decided to move we could share her room for the time being. That way I wouldn't have to buy a bed. But now, having been in Washington for only a handful of days, the plans have already changed to me sleeping on an air mattress.

Then there are the dogs. Of course, I had brought my one-year-old Cocker Spaniel, Dickens, Rachel had Henry, and Arizona had Betsy, a mix of black lab and something else. While I knew both Henry and Bets from having gone over to hang with them before I got Dickens, Henry and Betsy didn't know Dickens, so bringing a new dog that was practically still a puppy into a new house was turning out to be a struggle. Henry growls at Dickens whenever he goes into Rachel's bedroom, and Betsy growls at both Dickens AND me whenever we go into Arizona's room to go to bed. Dickens can't play with his toys because the other dogs get jealous, and during feeding time I have to hover over Dickens to make sure he gets enough food to eat.

# WMRG

Wenatchee Mountain Roller Girls is the name of my new roller derby league in Washington. I had skated with the league a few times over the summer while visiting Rachel. When I arrived in Washington, their regular travel team season was winding down with only a few bouts left on the schedule. Since the league was smaller, it didn't consist of home teams but rather just two travel teams.

Because of schoolwork, Rachel is unable to accompany me on my first night of skating with WMRG. When I arrive at the high school gymnasium where the league practices a few nights per week, I'm greeted by a couple familiar faces I had seen over the summer. The girls are welcoming and excited that I have decided to skate with their league.

As I begin putting on my derby gear, one of the league skaters comes over to me with a packet of papers.

"Here are the usual waiver forms," she says, handing them to me. "Just sign on the lines. Looks like we have your WFTDA insurance number, so you're good there. Here's our Code of Conduct, which you might want to read later since it's kind of long. Oh, and here are your transfer papers."

I sign the Code of Conduct agreement form and the WFTDA insurance form, but pause when I reach the transfer paperwork. I glance over it and skim the bulleted lines that read: *Must have*

*played at least one year with previous league, receive letter of rec-*
*ommendation from former league* . . . yadda yadda yadda. As I
stare at the paper, an uneasy feeling settles in my gut. *What am I*
*doing out here? What am I thinking transferring leagues?* But, before these questions get off to a full start in my head, I silence
them with a nod and a signature on the dotted line.

# No Boozing

Since there isn't cable at Arizona and Rachel's, I decide to catch a few football games at a local sports bar one Sunday afternoon. The NFL season was already in full swing so not watching football seemed like a sin. I pull a chair up to the bar and order a large mug of Miller Lite. I haven't had a drop of booze in over a week, so I *really* need a beer. Rachel was planning to be on campus studying all afternoon, so she'd never have to know I had a drink. The first beer tastes amazing. And a little while later, so does the second beer. And the third. And the fourth.

I've got a good buzz going when I pull into my parking space at the townhouse. Rachel's car is back and, because I know I reek of beer, I quickly fumble through the glove compartment in search of a piece of gum or a mint or anything that will cover up my beer breath. I settle on a mini Hershey bar I find beneath the passenger seat. I have no idea how long the deformed piece of candy has been under there, how many cycles of *thaw, melt, freeze, repeat* it's been through, but at this moment death-by-chocolate seems more welcoming than death-by-derby-wife if Rachel finds out I'm drunk.

I walk up the stairs and into the hallway and Rachel greets me from her bedroom.

"Hi," I say with a wave while turning in to Arizona's room. My plan is to grab clean clothes and head into the bathroom for a long, long, *long* detox shower.

"Hey, where have you been?" Rachel yells across the hallway.

"Ah," I say from inside the closet, "I stopped downtown to watch some football."

"Oh, that's fun," she says.

"Yeah, what have you been up to?" I ask, trying to change the subject. I bundle up my clean clothes, walk into the hallway, and flick on the bathroom light. I see Rachel sitting at her computer, likely working on school stuff.

"I was at the library pretty much all day," she says turning from her computer screen to look at me. "Hey, did you have anything to drink?" she asks as I'm about to disappear into the bathroom.

I pause for a moment, biting my lower lip. I want to say that I just had a Coke, but for reasons unknown a wave of Catholic guilt suddenly floods through my veins and I reply, "Yeah, I had a beer," and close the bathroom door.

*Two hours later . . .*

"Sam, you remember our deal?" Rachel says to me in the kitchen. She stands in her pajamas, ready for bed. I sit in front of my laptop that's resting atop the small kitchen table.

"Ah . . ." I say hesitantly.

"The deal that you weren't going to drink when you came out here," Rachel says before I can finish my sentence.

"Yeah."

"Well I was serious about it. If you want to live out here with me and Arizona you can't drink."

"What if I want a beer?" I can feel my blood beginning to boil. I hate when anyone tries to tell me what I can and can't do. "I mean, what if I just want to have a beer?"

"That's just it, you can never have *just one*," Rachel says looking me in the eyes.

"I can too have just one and be fine with it," I say, though I no longer believe it.

"Before you moved out here we had a deal and now you've been out here for what, a week, and you're already out drinking."

"Well, I didn't know I wasn't going to be able to drink AT ALL," I reply sensing my cheeks are growing red. I know Rachel is right and that I'm violating my part of the deal.

"Sam, all I'm saying is that if you're going to stay out here and live with us, you CAN'T DRINK," she says shaking her head.

"Not even a little bit? Like a beer?"

"No, not even a little bit."

When Rachel goes upstairs to bed, I continue to sit at my computer. I don't know who to talk to or how to vent my anger. Normally these types of emotions are nipped in the butt with a few drinks. I feel lost so I log on to Facebook and type a long message to Skuggs, a skater at FMDG who is currently the league's liaison. I explain to her everything that has just happened between Rachel and me.

# A Blue Book

"Sammi, and I'm an alcoholic."

Chorus (nodding heads): "Hi Sammi."

"Ahh, I don't really know where to start. This is my first time talking at one of these things. I moved out here from Fargo. I guess I needed a change. I'm living with a couple friends who are going to grad school out here, so that works out pretty well. My friends think I have an alcohol problem. I guess I like to go out and party and stuff, but who doesn't? But it's not like I sit around by myself and drink into oblivion or anything like that. I only drink socially. My one friend says I can't live with them if I'm drinking. So I guess I'm not supposed to drink . . . because I have a drinking problem. That's all I have to say about that."

Dalton pats me on the back and whispers, "Good job."

I glance around the room and observe the buffet of people sitting in a circle. One man looks tired, his face wrinkled and his mouth fixed in a stoic frown. Another man wears a cowboy hat and eats from a large bowl of Instant Ramen Noodles. A lady wearing a Mickey Mouse sweatshirt is talking now and she smiles here and there. Glancing across the table, I notice a large blue book in front of the frowning man. Looking further down the table I see a few more blue books in front of other people. *How did I ever end up here? Of all places?*

The short answer is that Rachel asked me if I would be willing to get help for my problem. I had agreed and the following day she hooked me up with one of her Merby friends, Dalton, who had been sober for a few years. I had met Dalton a couple times at WMRG practices because his wife skated for the league, so I recognized him when we met outside in a downtown parking lot. He informed me that this AA meeting was the noonday meeting, and that there was also a morning and an evening meeting each day of the week.

At the end of the meeting, I learn the blue book is titled *Alcoholics Anonymous*.

"Do you have one of these books?" I ask Dalton while picking one up. The book is thick and heavy and doesn't boast a shiny jacket.

"Yes. Actually I have one at home," Dalton replies. "It's a really good reference, and it's used a lot in meetings. Different meetings focus on different topics of AA, like one meeting might focus on something from the book, while another meeting might focus more on just talking."

I nod, thinking maybe I should get one. "How much does the book cost?" I ask Dalton.

"Hey Sarah," Chris says toward the woman wearing the Mickey Mouse sweatshirt. "How much is a book?"

"Hang on a second," Sarah says. She walks over to a man sitting behind a desk, says something to him, and he hands her a key. Sarah smiles at Dalton and me as she walks across the room, unlocks a large brown cabinet, and takes out a blue book. She walks over to me and, placing the book in my hands, says, "This one is for you, on the house."

# A Problem

When I get home from the coffee shop I'm told Dickens peed. I find it strange because I've only been gone a couple hours and I'd taken him out right before I left. I feel bad that he peed because he went on Henry's little bed *and* Rachel's leg. So now, once again, I feel like a problem. Rachel tells me to spray odor remover on Henry's bed, so I do, but it seems pointless because it's going in the washing machine anyway.

Rachel never returned my text from the coffee shop. I'd asked her if she wanted me to bring anything home for her — a mocha, a bagel, a cookie? But she never answered. A simple "yes" or "no" or "thanks for asking" would've been fine.

I feel ignored. And now, with Dickens peeing — which I still think is odd because I'd left him at home for eight hours or more when I was in Fargo and he never had any accidents then — Rachel doesn't have much to say to me. She's always busy and I feel we never have any time to connect. And when we do have something to talk about, I feel like it's in regards to something I've done wrong, or, now in this case, something my dog has done wrong.

# If I Could Afford to See a Psychologist

I'd like to share with a psychologist the ridiculousness of not being able to see a psychologist because I don't have insurance and can't pay any bills up front. I just moved to a new area of the country. I've applied to job after job and I haven't received an email back from anyone. I don't know anyone in town. My roommates are always gone at school. I got bitched out the other night for being inconsiderate because I left my dog at home without asking if anyone could watch him. I feel like I'm on the verge of getting in trouble for things I have no idea I'm about to get in trouble for. It was different when I was drinking. I knew I'd get into trouble after too many beers. But at that point in time I already had planned out in my mind the apologies I'd have to make in a hung-over state of mind the following day. So now I go to AA meetings. And now because I can't drink I can't seem to control my emotions. I cry. Sometimes it's because I have no money. Sometimes it's because I miss my roller derby team in Fargo. Sometimes it's because one of my roommates refers to my dog as either "fucker" or "little shit." Even though he is a dog, I still think he understands things, and I don't want him feeling bad about himself. My other roommate called my dog "annoying." This made me cry. He is my best friend. Yes, he is a puppy and has lots of energy, but isn't that expected of a puppy? He hasn't yet been burdened by the crappiness of life. Maybe that's why I get upset when my roommates call him names — because I am subconsciously trying to protect him from the cruelties of life. I have a degree. I almost have a master's. Yet, I am jobless. I am tired. I could hardly keep my eyes open during the noon AA meeting I attended today. I am stressed, and I can't drink to cope with it and that stresses me out. I sent an email to the campus counseling center in town asking if, because I was enrolled as a grad student in a different university, it would at all be possible to meet with a counselor on campus. No one ever replied. I thought moving was supposed to be a good thing. Sure, I've started going to AA meetings and I feel a connection there. I do, however, have a nagging desire to drink a beer. By a beer I mean a twelve pack. Bottled. I feel like I am a problem for my roommates. I feel like just being around in general is a problem. I feel like I'm going to get yelled at or get a cold shoulder for no particular reason. It's nothing I can prevent; it's just going to happen. I joined the roller derby team out here and just as I'm starting to get in the swing of practice, it's the end of the season and regular practices won't start up again until January. The season out here is the complete opposite of back home. The more I need derby the further it gets away from me. I feel that way with a lot of things. The more I crave affection and warmth from someone the further away it seems to get. The more I crave a job, the harder it is to find one. There are jobs everywhere to be found when you're not looking. But as soon as you start looking they vanish. Nobody ever returns your call or email. So today I called the psychologist-counseling place in town and said I'd like to get in to see someone because I had just moved to the area. I said I didn't yet have a job and asked if they did any type of pro-rating. The lady on the other end of the line said no, no pro-rating. I asked how much a visit to see someone would cost. First I'd have to have an evaluation, which would be fifty-eight dollars. I half-stopped listening at that point because fifty-eight dollars is a lot of money to a person who has no money. There was mention of something about seeing someone for $100, then another something that was $215. I told her thanks for the information. But what I really wanted to tell her was that it seemed unfair that a person who is down and out because she can't find a job and she can't have a beer and she can't please her roommates and she doesn't know anyone else in town can't get help because she lacks the green to pay for the help. But I decided not to tell her this because she wouldn't care anyway since she probably had health insurance thanks to sitting behind a clinic desk and taking phone calls from people like me who can't afford medical attention because they have no desk to sit behind and no phone to answer and no check that arrives via mail every other Friday.

# A Time to Go

It all happens so quickly. Earlier in the day, Rachel and I had met up for lunch and had chatted about how things were going. I told her I had finally gotten a response back from a job I had applied for and that I had an interview scheduled for the following week. I told her about the upcoming AA dinner event that was on Friday night. I had been given a free ticket by someone at a meeting and was told I should definitely attend because the food was delicious.

That evening when Rachel came home from school, she was in a better-than-usual mood. We had decided to head over to the grocery store to grab a frozen pizza and a movie for the night. I was excited because she was finally taking an evening off from schoolwork, finally taking an evening to hang out together on the couch. While the pizza was baking, we took the dogs for a short walk. I had decided to take Betsy on our walk since Arizona would be on campus late. It had rained earlier in the day, and the streets were filled with puddles.

When we got home from the walk, Rachel asked if I wouldn't mind giving Betsy a quick bath. I happily agreed because I knew when Arizona came home she'd be all excited to be greeted by a fresh smelling Betsy.

I walk down the stairs after Betsy's bath and ask if the pizza is done because it smells amazing. There's no reply as I come around the corner into the living room. The lights are off and Rachel is lying on the couch watching a show on Netflix.

"Bets is extra clean," I announce.

Rachel still doesn't reply. I go into the kitchen to grab a slice of pizza and sit down in front of my computer at the kitchen table. Rachel continues to sit in silence and I look over to her, wondering what's up.

"Is something wrong?" I ask, tilting my head trying to peek over the couch. I can't see Rachel's face because the lights are off. "Hey, are you all right?"

"I'm fine," she says with a snap.

I pick up my iPhone to see if I have any missed texts. When I swipe my thumb to unlock the phone, instead of the main screen popping up, a private Facebook message opens. I stare at it for a second, confused because I don't remember leaving any messages open. Suddenly a weight hits my gut and a sick feeling comes over me. *Oh my God, Rachel read my messages.* I look at the message more closely and realize it's one between me and Skuggs back in Fargo. The screen is scrolled down to a point in the message that talks about me not being sure I can live with Rachel anymore.

"Hey," I look up from my phone and over toward the couch. "Ah, did you read my Facebook messages?"

There's no reply, so I ask again. "Rachel, did you read my messages?"

"Sam, I think it's time for you to leave," Rachel says from the couch. I feel sick again as I stand up and walk toward her. She's lying on the couch and I can tell she's been crying.

I crouch down on the floor next to her. "Did you read my messages?"

She begins to sob, "Sam, I think it's time for you to leave."

My eyes fill with tears. "Those were private messages on my phone," I say knowing full well she read them.

"This isn't working, you living out here. It was supposed to be fun but it's not," Rachel says.

"I know it's been rough and that I've been moody and irritated because I can't drink," I wipe away a tear, "But I'm working on it and I haven't had a drink in twenty-nine days."

Rachel looks at me with hurt eyes and says, "It's time for you to leave."

I'm so upset that I take Dickens and we drive across town. I call my sister and tell her everything that has just happened. I had been talking to Jen on a regular basis while being in Washington. She knew I was having a hard time with my living situation. After listening to my story, she agrees that things aren't good and that Washington probably isn't the best place for me to be right now.

"Listen Sambo," Jen says over the phone. "I've been talking to John lately about your whole situation, and we've decided that if you want to, you're more than welcome to come live with us."

I cry harder because it's the kindest thing I've heard in a while.

"John and I both think living in Washington isn't the best for you right now. You've said you can't find a job, you hardly ever get to see Rachel, you're not skating right now, and you're trying to get sober, which I think is awesome. It would be good for you and D to come to the Cities. The job market here is good, you can live with us and save up some money, there's roller derby here, and you can live with your favorite sister."

"Who says you're my favorite?" I joke through a sob.

"Actually," I say wiping a tear from my face, "the other day I was online looking at a derby league in Minneapolis."

"See, I told you there was derby here," she says.

"Well, I knew there was, and I watched this league play a couple years ago. They're called North Star Roller Girls."

# Dickens and Me

It's been fourteen hours since Rachel and I talked. I carry things from the townhouse out to my car, trying to make everything squish in the way it did on the move out. Snow is falling on this mid-November Saturday, and I brush it off Dickens's feet before I buckle him into the back seat.

I run back inside to grab a couple more things and Rachel stops me in the hallway. "Got it all packed up?" she asks.

I don't say anything and walk by her to grab another load of my things.

"Sam, don't be like this," she says. I stop and turn to her. Her eyes are puffy and she's on the verge of crying, which makes me want to cry.

I set my armful of stuff down and walk in between her open arms for a hug. We stand embraced in each other's arms. She cries. I cry. This is the closest I've felt to her during the six weeks I've been here.

"None of this is your fault," I say. "It's not your fault; it just didn't work out right now."

I pull back and look her in the eyes, "I mean it," I say. Rachel nods in agreement. "I guess for some reason it's not meant to be right now."

Rachel helps me carry the remaining items to my car. She leans in through the driver side and pets Dickens on the head.

"Well, I'm sure Dickens will be excited to stay in another hotel room again," I say. "On the way out here, whenever my mom and I would stop for the night, he was always thrilled. He loved jumping between one bed and the other."

Rachel chuckles and smiles again. "Shoot me a text when you get to where you're stopping for the night," she says and gives me another hug.

As I pull onto I-90 East, the mountains are covered in a fresh blanket of snow. I glance back at Dickens in my rearview mirror. He sits upright, looking out the front window.

"Ready to head back home Buddy-Boy?" I stretch my free arm back to him and scratch his chest. His face nudges my hand and he gives it a warm lick.

"Me too."

# GLOSSARY OF DERBY-NESS

**25 in 5** n. A Basic Skills test in which a skater is required to skate twenty-five consecutive laps within a five-minute time period.

**Basic Skills** n. A WFTDA-recognized set of minimum skating requirements every roller derby skater must pass before she is allowed to bout.

**Blades2Quads** v. (roller blades to quad skates) **1.** The transition period from roller blades to roller skates. **2.** One of the make or break points in a derby girl's career in which a skater questions their center of gravity, tests the durability of their protective equipment, and challenges their own sanity.

**The Box** n. **1.** A 12 x 6 foot custom-made wooden structure in the middle of the Warehouse track that covers a gaping hole leading to Hades. **2.** A 12 x 6 foot custom-made wooden structure in the middle of the Warehouse track that covers a gaping hole leading to Hades that is also used to hold everyone's shit—water bottles, crusty Band-Aids, tampons, a chewed piece of gum, somebody's sports bra, etc.

**The Déjà 500** v. Déjà Who's idea of a "fun" endurance drill where two skaters share the burden of skating a total of 210 laps around the flat track. Ex: "Ugh, we're doing the Déjà 500 tonight? I knew I should've stayed home."

**Derby Skinz** n. Extremely tight spandex shorts that leave nothing to the imagination.

**Flo-Ho** n. [\flow-hoe\] A derby skater who spends a longer than average amount of time on the floor. Ex: "Jeeze, Ya'll's Mom was falling all over the place tonight, she was such a flo-ho."

**Fresh Meat** n. A red slab of new derby girl who falls a lot, has yet to pass Basic Skills, and is completely clueless about roller derby.

**Giner-Shiner** adj. [\j-eye-ner \ sh-eye-ner\] A painful hit / later bruise to the va-jay-jay. Ex: [Player grabs crotch while rolling around on floor] "Oh man! Tool Pelt just gave me a giner-shiner!"

**Hungry Butt** n./v. [aka "vacuum butt"] **1.** (n.) Tight derby skins that get sucked up into a skater's butt. **2.** (v). The act of a skater's butt devouring or nomming on tightly fitted booty skins. Ex: "Did you see Missy Hit-Her's skins when she was jamming tonight? Jeeze, she sure had a hungry butt!"

**Merby** n. **1.** Men's Roller Derby. **2.** An organization of men who can't accept the obvious fact that the sport of roller derby is best played by women.

**Pandora's Box** n. **1.** An artifact in Greek mythology given to Pandora (first woman on earth) which, once opened, released evil into the world. **2.** Source of extensive but unforeseen troubles or problems. **3.** The FMDG Warehouse.

**T-stop** v. A basic roller derby stop that involves lining up the inside of one foot directly behind the opposite foot's heel (like a 90-degree angle) and using the back foot's wheels to stop. [When executed correctly, the skater's feet resemble an upside-down T.]

**Tenderized Meat** n. A bruised, battered, mallet-pounded red slab of new derby girl who has passed Basic Skills and is 99 percent clueless about roller derby.

**Tequila Pudding Shot** n. Strong and carefully concocted alcoholic shot set in ketchup containers (for easy distribution) made by Beer Biznatch the night before a bout. Ex: "Thowzzz Tequiiiila Poooding shoz'll fahck yewww up…"

# ACKNOWLEDGEMENTS

Huge thanks to NDSU Press, Suzzanne Kelley, and the publishing interns for making this book a reality. Thank you to the FM Derby Girls for taking a chance on a raw slab of Fresh Meat who, at first, couldn't perform even the most basic derby moves. Thanks to my family for all the love, support, strange stories, and (at times) inappropriate humor. Emily Krook, thanks for sharing your graphic design skills. North Star Roller Girls, thanks for helping me find the other side of derby. And Mom, thanks for never bailing on me . . . even during the worst of times.

# ABOUT THE AUTHOR

Sammi Jones got her start in roller derby in 2010 when she joined the Fargo Moorhead Derby Girls. She holds a Master of Fine Arts in Creative Writing from Minnesota State University Moorhead and has written for a variety of publications. She resides in the Minneapolis – St. Paul area where she works as an assistant editor for a trade magazine and skates for Minneapolis's North Star Roller Girls.

# ABOUT THE PRESS

North Dakota State University Press (NDSU Press) exists to stimulate and coordinate interdisciplinary regional scholarship. These regions include the Red River Valley, the state of North Dakota, the plains of North America (comprising both the Great Plains of the United States and the prairies of Canada), and comparable regions of other continents. We publish peer reviewed regional scholarship shaped by national and international events and comparative studies.

Neither topic nor discipline limits the scope of NDSU Press publications. We consider manuscripts in any field of learning. We define our scope, however, by a regional focus in accord with the press's mission. Generally, works published by NDSU Press address regional life directly, as the subject of study. Such works contribute to scholarly knowledge of region (that is, discovery of new knowledge) or to public consciousness of region (that is, dissemination of information, or interpretation of regional experience). Where regions abroad are treated, either for comparison or because of ties to those North American regions of primary concern to the press, the linkages are made plain.

For nearly three-quarters of a century, NDSU Press has published substantial trade books, but the line of publications is not limited to that genre. We also publish textbooks (at any level), reference books, anthologies, reprints, papers, proceedings, and monographs. The press also considers works of poetry or fiction, provided they are established regional classics or they promise to assume landmark or reference status for the region. We select biographical or autobiographical works carefully for their prospective contribution to regional knowledge and culture. All publications, in whatever genre, are of such quality and substance as to embellish the imprint of NDSU Press.

Our name changed to North Dakota State University Press in January 2016. Prior to that, and since 1950, we published as the North Dakota Institute for Regional Studies Press. We continue to operate under the umbrella of the North Dakota Institute for Regional Studies, located at North Dakota State University.